BLOOM'S

HOW TO WRITE ABOUT

Oscar Wilde

AMY WATKIN

Introduction by Harold Bloom

BLOOM'S
LITERARY CRITICISM
An imprint of Infobase Publishing

Bloom's How to Write about Oscar Wilde

Copyright © 2010 by Infobase Publishing
Introduction © 2010 by Harold Bloom

Bloom's Literary Criticism
An imprint of Infobase Publishing
132 West 31st Street
New York NY 10001

Library of Congress Cataloging-in-Publication Data
Watkin, Amy S.
    Bloom's how to write about Oscar Wilde / Amy Watkin ; introduction by Harold Bloom.
        p. cm.—(Bloom's how to write about literature)
    Includes bibliographical references and index.
    ISBN 978-1-60413-309-7
    1. Wilde, Oscar, 1854–1900—Criticism and interpretation. 2. Criticism—Authorship. I. Title. II. Title: How to write about Oscar Wilde. III. Series.
PR5824.W37 2009
828'.809—dc22   2009002041

Text design by Annie O'Donnell
Cover design by Alicia Post

Printed in the United States of America

MP MSRF 10 9 8 7 6 5 4 3 2 1

This book is printed on acid-free paper.

CONTENTS

SERIES
INTRODUCTION

BLOOM's How to Write about Literature series is designed to inspire students to write fine essays on great writers and their works. Each volume in the series begins with an introduction by Harold Bloom, meditating on the challenges and rewards of writing about the volume's subject author. The first chapter then provides detailed instructions on how to write a good essay, including how to find a thesis; how to develop an outline; how to write a good introduction, body text, and conclusion; how to cite sources; and more. The second chapter provides a brief overview of the issues involved in writing about the subject author and then a number of suggestions for paper topics, with accompanying strategies for addressing each topic. Succeeding chapters cover the author's major works.

The paper topics suggested within this book are open-ended, and the brief strategies provided are designed to give students a push forward in the writing process rather than a road map to success. The aim of the book is to pose questions, not answer them. Many different kinds of papers could result from each topic. As always, the success of each paper will depend completely on the writer's skill and imagination.

HOW TO WRITE ABOUT OSCAR WILDE: INTRODUCTION

by Harold Bloom

To write about Oscar Wilde, it is good to remember the principle of Jorge Luis Borges: Oscar was always right. Though hyperbole was Wilde's favorite trope, his overthrows remarkably and consistently do not fall beyond the mark. The Bloomian principle for reading Oscar is: Take his wit seriously and his high seriousness comically, for that is his essence. A man dying all too young, in exile, who can remark: "I am dying above my means," while murmuring that either the wallpaper or he must go, needs an alerted response.

Wilde is a great comic dramatist, particularly in *The Importance of Being Earnest*, and an important though not original critic. As the disciple of John Ruskin and Walter Pater, he popularizes their ideas without strongly modifying them. The dialogical *The Decay of Lying* is his salient critical contribution, and I myself owe a debt to his vision of the saving lie.

Aside from Pater and Ruskin, Wilde's authentic literary affinity is with the great Victorian nonsense writers Lewis Carroll and Edward Lear. Try reading side by side any of Wilde's stage comedies and the great *Alice* romances of Lewis Carroll, or juxtapose Oscar's critical dialogues with Edward Lear's *The Dong with the Luminous Nose* and *The Courtship of the Yonghy-Bonghy-Bo.*

Weirdly enough, though *The Ballad of Reading Gaol* too closely imitates the metrics and atmosphere of Coleridge's *The Rime of the Ancient Mariner*, Wilde's prison poem actually emanates from the realm of Lewis Carroll's mad quest-romance *The Hunting of the Snark*. Juxtapose the two, and the results will be surprising.

To sum it: We cannot be Wilde, as his genius is beyond us, but we need to be as Wildean as possible in writing about him. A conventional response will fail. Oscar *is* paradox and needs to be ambushed—by wily stratagems and (only apparently) lunatic juxtapositions.

HOW TO WRITE A GOOD ESSAY

By Laurie A. Sterling and Amy Watkin

WHILE THERE are many ways to write about literature, most assignments for high school and college English classes call for analytical papers. In these assignments, you are presenting your interpretation of a text to your reader. Your objective is to interpret the text's meaning in order to enhance your reader's understanding and enjoyment of the work. Without exception, strong papers about the meaning of a literary work are built upon a careful, close reading of the text or texts. Careful, analytical reading should always be the first step in your writing process. This volume provides models of such close, analytical reading, and these should help you develop your own skills as a reader and as a writer.

As the examples throughout this book demonstrate, attentive reading entails thinking about and evaluating the formal (textual) aspects of the author's works: theme, character, form, and language. In addition, when writing about a work, many readers choose to move beyond the text itself to consider the work's cultural context. In these instances, writers might explore the historical circumstances of the time period in which the work was written. Alternatively, they might examine the philosophies and ideas that a work addresses. Even in cases where writers explore a work's cultural context, though, papers must still address the more formal aspects of the work itself. A good interpretative essay that evaluates Oscar Wilde's use of the philosophy of hedonism in his novel *The Picture of Dorian Gray*, for example, cannot adequately address the author's treatment of the philosophy without firmly grounding this discussion in the book itself. In other

1

words, any analytical paper about a text, even one that seeks to evaluate the work's cultural context, must also have a firm handle on the work's themes, characters, and language. You must look for and evaluate these aspects of a work, then, as you read a text and as you prepare to write about it.

WRITING ABOUT THEMES

Literary themes are more than just topics or subjects treated in a work; they are attitudes or points about these topics that often structure other elements in a work. Writing about theme therefore requires that you not just identify a topic that a literary work addresses but also discuss what that work says about that topic. For example, if you were writing about the culture of the American South in William Faulkner's famous story "A Rose for Emily," you would need to discuss what Faulkner says, argues, or implies about that culture and its passing.

When you prepare to write about thematic concerns in a work of literature, you will probably discover that, like most works of literature, your text touches upon other themes in addition to its central theme. These secondary themes also provide rich ground for paper topics. A thematic paper on "A Rose for Emily" might consider gender or race in the story. While neither of these could be said to be the central theme of the story, they are clearly related to the passing of the "old South" and could provide plenty of good material for papers.

As you prepare to write about themes in literature, you might find a number of strategies helpful. After you identify a theme or themes in the story, you should begin by evaluating how other elements of the story—such as character, point of view, imagery, and symbolism—help develop the theme. You might ask yourself what your own responses are to the author's treatment of the subject matter. Do not neglect the obvious, either: What expectations does the title set up? How does the title help develop thematic concerns? Clearly, the title "A Rose for Emily" says something about the narrator's attitude toward the title character, Emily Grierson, and all she represents.

WRITING ABOUT CHARACTER

Generally, characters are essential components of fiction and drama. (This is not always the case, though; Ray Bradbury's "August 2026: There

Will Come Soft Rains" is technically a story without characters, at least any human characters.) Often, you can discuss character in poetry, as in T. S. Eliot's "The Love Song of J. Alfred Prufrock" or Robert Browning's "My Last Duchess." Many writers find that analyzing character is one of the most interesting and engaging ways to work with a piece of literature and to shape a paper. After all, characters generally are human, and we all know something about being human and living in the world. While it is always important to remember that these figures are not real people but creations of the writer's imagination, it can be fruitful to begin evaluating them as you might evaluate a real person. Often you can start with your own response to a character. Did you like or dislike the character? Did you sympathize with the character? Why or why not?

Keep in mind, though, that emotional responses like these are just starting places. To truly explore and evaluate literary characters, you need to return to the formal aspects of the text and evaluate how the author has drawn these characters. The 20th-century writer E. M. Forster coined the terms *flat* characters and *round* characters. Flat characters are static, one-dimensional characters who frequently represent a particular concept or idea. In contrast, round characters are fully drawn and much more realistic characters who frequently change and develop over the course of a work. Are the characters you are studying flat or round? What elements of the characters lead you to this conclusion? Why might the author have drawn characters like this? How does their development affect the meaning of the work? Similarly, you should explore the techniques the author uses to develop characters. Do we hear a character's own words, or do we hear only other characters' assessments of him or her? Or does the author use an omniscient or limited omniscient narrator to allow us access to the workings of the characters' minds? If so, how does that help develop the characterization? Often you can even evaluate the narrator as a character. How trustworthy are the opinions and assessments of the narrator? You should also think about characters' names. Do they mean anything? If you encounter a hero named Sophia or Sophie, you should probably think about her wisdom (or lack thereof), since *Sophia* means "wisdom" in Greek. Similarly, since the name *Sylvia* is derived from the word *sylvan,* meaning "of the wood," you might want to evaluate that character's relationship with nature. Once again, you might look to the title of the work. Does Herman Melville's "Bartleby, the Scrivener" signal anything about Bartleby himself? Is Bartleby adequately defined by his job as scrivener? Is this part of Melville's point? Pursuing questions like these can help you develop thorough papers about characters from psychological, sociological, or more formalistic perspectives.

WRITING ABOUT FORM AND GENRE

Genre, a word derived from French, means "type" or "class." Literary genres are distinctive classes or categories of literary composition. On the most general level, literary works can be divided into the genres of drama, poetry, fiction, and essays, yet within those genres there are classifications that are also referred to as genres. Tragedy and comedy, for example, are genres of drama. Epic, lyric, and pastoral are genres of poetry. *Form,* on the other hand, generally refers to the shape or structure of a work. There are many clearly defined forms of poetry that follow specific patterns of meter, rhyme, and stanza. Sonnets, for example, are poems that follow a fixed form of 14 lines. Sonnets generally follow one of two basic sonnet forms, each with its own distinct rhyme scheme. Haiku is another example of poetic form, traditionally consisting of three unrhymed lines of five, seven, and five syllables.

While you might think that writing about form or genre might leave little room for argument, many of these forms and genres are very fluid. Remember that literature is evolving and ever changing, and so are its forms. As you study poetry, you may find that poets, especially more modern poets, play with traditional poetic forms, bringing about new effects. Similarly, dramatic tragedy was once quite narrowly defined, but over the centuries playwrights have broadened and challenged traditional definitions, changing the shape of tragedy. When Arthur Miller wrote *Death of a Salesman,* many critics challenged the idea that tragic drama could encompass a common man like Willy Loman.

Evaluating how a work of literature fits into or challenges the boundaries of its form or genre can provide you with fruitful avenues of investigation. You might find it helpful to ask why the work does or does not fit into traditional categories. Why might Miller have thought it fitting to write a tragedy of the common man? Similarly, you might compare the content or theme of a work with its form. How well do they work together? Many of Emily Dickinson's poems, for instance, follow the meter of traditional hymns. While some of her poems seem to express traditional religious doctrines, many seem to challenge or strain against traditional conceptions of God and theology. What is the effect, then, of her use of traditional hymn meter?

WRITING ABOUT LANGUAGE, SYMBOLS, AND IMAGERY

No matter what the genre, writers use words as their most basic tool. Language is the most fundamental building block of literature. It is essential that you pay careful attention to the author's language and word choice as you read, reread, and analyze a text. Imagery is language that appeals to the senses. Most commonly, imagery appeals to our sense of vision, creating a mental picture, but authors also use language that appeals to our other senses. Images can be literal or figurative. Literal images use sensory language to describe an actual thing. In the broadest terms, figurative language uses one thing to speak about something else. For example, if I call my boss a snake, I am not saying that he is literally a reptile. Instead, I am using figurative language to communicate my opinions about him. Since we think of snakes as sneaky, slimy, and sinister, I am using the concrete image of a snake to communicate these abstract opinions and impressions.

The two most common figures of speech are similes and metaphors. Both are comparisons between two apparently dissimilar things. Similes are explicit comparisons using the words *like* or *as*; metaphors are implicit comparisons. To return to the previous example, if I say, "My boss, Bob, was waiting for me when I showed up to work five minutes late today—the snake!" I have constructed a metaphor. Writing about his experiences fighting in World War I, Wilfred Owen begins his poem "Dulce et decorum est," with a string of similes: "Bent double, like old beggars under sacks, / Knock-kneed, coughing like hags, we cursed through sludge." Owen's goal was to undercut clichéd notions that war and dying in battle were glorious. Certainly, comparing soldiers to coughing hags and to beggars underscores his point.

"Fog," a short poem by Carl Sandburg, provides a clear example of a metaphor. Sandburg's poem reads:

The fog comes
on little cat feet.

It sits looking
over harbor and city
on silent haunches
and then moves on.

Notice how effectively Sandburg conveys surprising impressions of the fog by comparing two seemingly disparate things—the fog and a cat.

Symbols, by contrast, are things that stand for, or represent, other things. Often they represent something intangible, such as concepts or ideas. In everyday life we use and understand symbols easily. Babies at christenings and brides at weddings wear white to represent purity. Think, too, of a dollar bill. The paper itself has no value in and of itself. Instead, that paper bill is a symbol of something else, the precious metal in a nation's coffers. Symbols in literature work similarly. Authors use symbols to evoke more than a simple, straightforward, literal meaning. Characters, objects, and places can all function as symbols. Famous literary examples of symbols include Moby Dick, the white whale of Herman Melville's novel, and the scarlet *A* of Nathaniel Hawthorne's *The Scarlet Letter*. As both of these symbols suggest, a literary symbol cannot be adequately defined or explained by any one meaning. Hester Prynne's Puritan community clearly intends her scarlet *A* as a symbol of her adultery, but as the novel progresses, even her own community reads the letter as representing not just *adultery*, but *able, angel,* and a host of other meanings.

Writing about imagery and symbols requires close attention to the author's language. To prepare a paper on symbolism or imagery in a work, identify and trace the images and symbols and then try to draw some conclusions about how they function. Ask yourself how any symbols or images help contribute to the themes or meanings of the work. What connotations do they carry? How do they affect your reception of the work? Do they shed light on characters or settings? A strong paper on imagery or symbolism will thoroughly consider the use of figures in the text and will try to reach some conclusions about how or why the author uses them.

WRITING ABOUT HISTORY AND CONTEXT

As noted above, it is possible to write an analytical paper that also considers the work's context. After all, the text was not created in a vacuum. The author lived and wrote in a specific time period and in a specific cultural context and, like all of us, was shaped by that environment. Learning more about the historical and cultural circumstances that surround the author and the work can help illuminate a text and provide you with productive material for a paper. Remember, though, that when you write analytical papers, you should use the context to illuminate the text. Do not lose sight of your goal—to interpret the meaning of the literary work. Use historical or philosophical research as a tool to develop your textual evaluation.

Thoughtful readers often consider how history and culture affected the author's choice and treatment of his or her subject matter. Investigations into the history and context of a work could examine the work's relation to specific historical events, such as the Salem witch trials in 17th-century Massachusetts or the restoration of Charles to the British throne in 1660. Bear in mind that historical context is not limited to politics and world events. While knowing about the Vietnam War is certainly helpful in interpreting much of Tim O'Brien's fiction, and some knowledge of the prison system in England clearly illuminates the dynamics of Oscar Wilde's *The Ballad of Reading Gaol*, historical context also entails the fabric of daily life. Examining a text in light of gender roles, race relations, class boundaries, or working conditions can give rise to thoughtful and compelling papers. Exploring the conditions of equality for women in 19th-century England, for example, can provide a particularly effective avenue for writing about Wilde's *The Importance of Being Earnest*.

You can begin thinking about these issues by asking broad questions at first. What do you know about the time period and about the author? What does the editorial apparatus in your text tell you? These might be starting places. Similarly, when specific historical events or dynamics are particularly important to understanding a work but might be somewhat obscure to modern readers, textbooks usually provide notes to explain historical background. These are a good place to start. With this information, ask yourself how these historical facts and circumstances might have affected the author, the presentation of theme, and the presentation of character. How does knowing more about the work's specific historical context illuminate the work? To take a well-known example, understanding the complex attitudes toward slavery during the time Mark Twain wrote *Adventures of Huckleberry Finn* should help you begin to examine issues of race in the text. Additionally, you might compare these attitudes to those of the time in which the novel was set. How might this comparison affect your interpretation of a work written after the abolition of slavery but set before the Civil War?

WRITING ABOUT PHILOSOPHY AND IDEAS

Philosophical concerns are closely related to both historical context and thematic issues. Like historical investigation, philosophical research can provide a useful tool as you analyze a text. For example, an investigation of the social classes in Wilde's England might lead you to a topic on the philosophical doctrine of moral absolutism in *Lady Windermere's Fan.* Many other works explore philosophies and ideas quite explicitly. Mary Shelley's famous novel *Frankenstein,* for example, explores John Locke's tabula rasa theory of human knowledge as she portrays the intellectual and emotional development of Victor Frankenstein's creature. As this example indicates, philosophical issues are somewhat more abstract than investigations of theme or historical context. Some other examples of philosophical issues include human free will, the formation of human identity, the nature of sin, or questions of ethics.

Writing about philosophy and ideas might require some outside research, but usually the notes or other material in your text will provide you with basic information and often footnotes and bibliographies suggest places you can go to read further about the subject. If you have identified a philosophical theme that runs through a text, you might ask yourself how the author develops this theme. Look at character development and the interactions of characters, for example. Similarly, you might examine whether the narrative voice in a work of fiction addresses the philosophical concerns of the text.

WRITING COMPARISON AND CONTRAST ESSAYS

Finally, you might find that comparing and contrasting the works or techniques of an author provides a useful tool for literary analysis. A comparison and contrast essay might compare two characters or themes in a single work, or it might compare the author's treatment of a theme in two works. It might also contrast methods of character development or analyze an author's differing treatment of a philosophical concern in two works. Writing comparison and contrast essays, though, requires some special consideration. While they generally provide you with plenty of material to use, they also come with a built-in trap: the laundry list. These papers often become mere lists of connections between the works. As this chapter will discuss, a strong thesis must make an assertion that you want to prove or validate. A strong comparison/contrast thesis, then, needs to comment on the significance of the similarities and differences you observe. It is not enough merely to assert that the works contain similarities and differences. You might, for example, assert why the similarities and differences are important and explain how they illuminate the works' treatment of theme. Remember, too, that a thesis should not be a statement of the obvious. A comparison/contrast paper that focuses only on very obvious similarities or differences does little to illuminate the connections between the works. Often, an effective method of shaping a strong thesis and argument is to begin your paper by noting the similarities between the works but then to develop a thesis that asserts how these apparently similar elements are different. If, for example, you observe that Emily Dickinson wrote a number of poems about spiders, you might analyze how she uses spider imagery differently in two poems. Similarly, many scholars have noted that Hawthorne created many "mad scientist" characters, men who are so devoted to their science or their art that they lose perspective on all else. A good thesis comparing two of these characters—Aylmer of "The Birth-mark" and Dr. Rappaccini of "Rappaccini's Daughter," for example—might initially identify both characters as examples of Hawthorne's mad scientist type but then argue that their motivations for scientific experimentation differ. If you strive to analyze the similarities or differences, discuss significances, and move beyond the obvious, your paper should bypass the laundry list trap.

PREPARING TO WRITE

Armed with a clear sense of your task—illuminating the text—and with an understanding of theme, character, language, history, and philosophy, you are ready to approach the writing process. Remember that good writing is grounded in good reading and that close reading takes time, attention, and more than one reading of your text. Read for comprehension first. As you go back and review the work, mark the text to chart the details of the work as well as your reactions. Highlight important passages, repeated words, and image patterns. "Converse" with the text through marginal notes. Mark turns in the plot, ask questions, and make observations about characters, themes, and language. If you are reading from a book that does not belong to you, keep a record of your reactions in a journal or notebook. If you have read a work of literature carefully, paying attention to both the text and the context of the work, you have a leg up on the writing process. Admittedly, at this point, your ideas are probably very broad and undefined, but you have taken an important first step toward writing a strong paper.

Your next step is to focus, to take a broad, perhaps fuzzy, topic and define it more clearly. Even a topic provided by your instructor will need to be focused appropriately. Remember that good writers make the topic their own. There are a number of strategies—often called "invention"—that you can use to develop your own focus. In one such strategy, called *freewriting*, you spend 10 minutes or so just writing about your topic without referring back to the text or your notes. Write whatever comes to mind; the important thing is that you just keep writing. Often this process allows you to develop fresh ideas or approaches to your subject matter. You could also try *brainstorming*: Write down your topic and then list all the related points or ideas you can think of. Include questions, comments, words, important passages or events, and anything else that comes to mind. Let one idea lead to another. In the related technique of *clustering*, or *mapping*, write your topic on a sheet of paper and write related ideas around it. Then list related subpoints under each of these main ideas. Many people then draw arrows to show connections between points. This technique helps you narrow your topic and can also help you organize your ideas. Similarly, asking journalistic questions—Who? What? Where? When? Why? and How?—can develop ideas for topic development.

Thesis Statements

Once you have developed a focused topic, you can begin to think about your thesis statement, the main point or purpose of your paper. It is imperative that you craft a strong thesis; otherwise, your paper will likely be little more than random, disorganized observations about the text. Think of your thesis statement as a kind of road map for your paper. It tells your reader where you are going and how you are going to get there.

To craft a good thesis, you must keep a number of things in mind. First, as the title of this subsection indicates, your paper's thesis should be a statement, an assertion about the text that you want to prove or validate. Beginning writers often formulate a question that they attempt to use as a thesis. For example, a writer exploring the gender distinctions in Wilde's *The Importance of Being Earnest* might ask, Is Wilde supporting female characters or making fun of them? While a question like this is a good strategy to use in the invention process to help narrow your topic and find your thesis, it cannot serve as the thesis statement because it does not tell your reader what you want to assert about your theme. You might shape this question into a thesis by instead proposing an answer to that question: Oscar Wilde fourned a wealth of hypocrisy in some of the feminists who championed the cause of the "New Woman." *The Importance of Being Earnest* provides a perfect battleground for such a subject. The characters of Cecily and Gwendolen in Wilde's comedic masterpiece are witty satirizations of this emerging concept of the Victorian era. Notice that this thesis provides an initial plan or structure for the rest of the paper, and notice, too, that the thesis statement does not necessarily have to fit into one sentence. After discussing the concept of the New Woman, you could examine the ways in which the idea of the New Woman is presented as inevitable in this play and then theorize about what Wilde is saying about women more generally.

Second, remember that a good thesis makes an assertion that you need to support. In other words, a good thesis does not state the obvious. If you tried to formulate a thesis about inequality by simply saying, Women are important in *The Importance of Being Earnest*, you have done nothing but rephrase the obvious. Since Wilde's play is centered on more than one woman with her own agenda, there would be no point in spending three to five pages supporting that assertion. You might try to develop a thesis from that point by asking yourself some further questions: What does it mean when any given character implies that women are merely decorative? Does the play seem to indicate that women and men are unequal in most ways? Does it present womanhood as an advantage in this world of such strict societal rules, or is womanhood presented as a source of vulnerability? Such a line of questioning might lead you to a more viable thesis, like the one in the preceding paragraph.

As the comparison with the road map also suggests, your thesis should appear near the beginning of the paper. In relatively short papers (three to six pages) the thesis almost always appears in the first paragraph. Some writers fall into the trap of saving their thesis for the end, trying to provide a surprise or a big moment of revelation, as if to say, for example, "TA-DA! I've just proved that in *An Ideal Husband* Wilde uses the snake brooch to symbolize Mrs. Cheveley's true character." Placing a thesis at the end of an essay can seriously mar the essay's effectiveness. If you fail to define your essay's point and purpose clearly at the beginning, your reader will find it difficult to assess the clarity of your argument and understand the points you are making. When your argument comes as a surprise at the end, you force your reader to reread your essay in order to assess its logic and effectiveness.

Finally, you should avoid using the first person ("I") as you present your thesis. Though it is not strictly wrong to write in the first person, it is difficult to do so gracefully. While writing in the first person, beginning writers often fall into the trap of writing self-reflexive prose (writing *about* their paper *in* their paper). Often this leads to the most dreaded of opening lines: "In this paper I am going to discuss . . ." Not only does this self-reflexive voice make for very awkward prose, it frequently allows writers to boldly announce a topic while completely avoiding a thesis statement. An example might be a paper that begins as follows: Oscar Wilde's The Importance of Being Earnest takes place in the fashionable parts of London and the English countryside, where the men cavort under various pseudonyms. In this paper I am going to discuss how the women in the play react to this. The author of this paper has done little more than announce a general topic for the paper (the reaction of women to the men's antics). While the last sentence might be a thesis, the writer fails to present an opinion about the significance of the reaction. To improve this "thesis," the writer would need to back up a couple of steps. First, the announced topic of the paper is too broad; it largely summarizes the events in the story, without saying anything about the ideas in the story. The writer should highlight what she considers the meaning of the story: What is the story about? The writer might conclude that the men's antics create feelings of inadequacy in the women. From here, the author could select the means by which Wilde communicates these ideas and then begin to craft a specific thesis. A writer who chooses to explore the symbols of frustration that are associated with fire might, for example, craft a thesis that reads, In *The Importance of Being Earnest*, Oscar Wilde characterizes Cecily and Gwendolen as witty satirizations of the emerging Victorian concept of the New Woman.

Outlines

While developing a strong, thoughtful thesis early in your writing process should help focus your paper, outlining provides an essential tool for logically shaping that paper. A good outline helps you see—and develop—the relationships among the points in your argument and assures you that your paper flows logically and coherently. Outlining not only helps place your points in a logical order but also helps you subordinate supporting points, weed out any irrelevant points, and decide if there are any necessary points that are missing from your argument. Most of us are familiar with formal outlines that use numerical and letter designations for each point. However, there are different types of outlines; you may find that an informal outline is a more useful tool for you. What is important, though, is that you spend the time to develop some sort of outline—formal or informal.

Remember that an outline is a tool to help you shape and write a strong paper. If you do not spend sufficient time planning your supporting points and shaping the arrangement of those points, you will most likely construct a vague, unfocused outline that provides little, if any, help with the writing of the paper. Consider the following example.

Thesis: In *The Importance of Being Earnest*, Oscar Wilde characterizes Cecily and Gwendolen as witty satirizations of the emerging Victorian concept of the New Woman.

I. Introduction and thesis

II. Gwendolen the flirt

III. Sarah Grand

IV. Jack Worthing

V. Cecily and Miss Prism

       A. Education
       B. Class
       C. Female solidarity
       D. Algernon

   VI. Conclusion
       A. Wilde provides several examples of the New
          Woman in *The Importance of Being Earnest,*
          particularly through the characters of
          Cecily, Gwendolen, and Miss Prism.

This outline has a number of flaws. First, the major topics labeled with the Roman numerals are not arranged in a logical order. If the paper's focus is on Gwendolen, the writer should establish the particulars of her character before discussing how flirting plays a role in her relationships with men. Similarly, the thesis makes no reference to Sarah Grand, but the writer includes her name as a major section of the outline. The writer could, however, include Sarah Grand in terms of her definition of the New Woman. As one of the main male characters in the play, Jack Worthing may well have a place in the essay being proposed, but the writer fails to provide details about his place in the argument. Third, the writer includes Algernon's character as one of the lettered items in section V. Letters A, B, and C all refer to specific instances in which the concept of the New Woman will be discussed; Algernon does not belong in this list. A fourth problem is the inclusion of a section A in section VI. An outline should not include an A without a B, a 1 without a 2, and so forth. The final problem with this outline is the overall lack of detail. None of the sections provides much information about the content of the argument, and it seems likely that the writer has not given sufficient thought to the content of the paper.

A better start to this outline might be the following:

Thesis: In *The Importance of Being Earnest,* Oscar Wilde
characterizes Cecily and Gwendolen as witty satirizations
of the emerging Victorian concept of the New Woman.

   I. Introduction and thesis

  II. Sarah Grand

A. Grand's definition of the New Woman
B. Wilde and Grand's disagreements
C. Satirizing Grand's ideas

III. Gwendolen the flirt
    A. Traveling alone
    B. Education

IV. Conflicts between Gwendolen and Cecily
    A. Different versions of the New Woman?
    B. Class issues

V. Cecily and Miss Prism
    A. Education
    B. Female solidarity

VI. Conclusion
    A. Gwendolen and Cecily, through their unwitting comic exploits, have provided perfect satirizations of the New Woman. If my connection is true, Wilde has exacted his revenge on the "aesthetic"-loathing Sarah Grand for more than a century.

    B. His ability to subtly point out hypocrisy in the context of the Victorian era was impeccable. We will continue to enjoy the exploits and antics of these characters for centuries to come.

An outline like this could be shaped into an even more useful tool if the writer fleshed out the argument by providing specific examples from the text to support each point. Once you have listed your main point and your supporting ideas, develop this raw material by listing related supporting ideas and material under each of those main headings. From there, arrange the material in subsections and order the material logically.

For example, you might begin with one of the theses cited above: In *The Importance of Being Earnest*, Oscar Wilde characterizes

Cecily and Gwendolen as witty satirizations of the emerging Victorian concept of the New Woman. As noted above, this thesis already gives you the beginning of an organization: Start by providing the necessary background about the New Woman and Wilde's views, and then explain how Wilde presents his female characters for the express purpose of satirizing a particular concept of the New Woman. You might begin your outline, then, with four topic headings: (1) Sarah Grand's definitions of the New Woman, (2) Wilde's possible conflicts with Grand and her ideas, (3) Gwendolen and Cecily as examples, and (4) How such information influences our understanding of Wilde's intentions. Under each of those headings you could list ideas that support the particular point. Be sure to include references to parts of the text that help build your case.

An informal outline might look like this:

Thesis: In *The Importance of Being Earnest*, Oscar Wilde characterizes Cecily and Gwendolen as witty satirizations of the emerging Victorian concept of the New Woman.

1. Introduction and thesis

2. Sarah Grand's definitions of the New Woman
   - Created the label in 1894
   - Woman's life should center on civic duty
   - Critic of the aesthetic movement
   - Disapproved of the public New Woman concept that emerged

3. Wilde's possible conflicts with Grand and her ideas
   - Disagreement over aestheticism
   - "Moral" scandal
   - Awareness of each other's work and ideas

4. Gwendolen and Cecily as examples
   - Gwendolen's immodest flirting
   - Gwendolen traveling alone
     - "For women of that era, travel seems to have been the individual gesture

of the housebound, male-dominated,
very proper lady. . . . [Traveling,]
she could enjoy a freedom of action
unthinkable at home. (Holcomb 1)
    ○ Travel equated with control of one's
own time
  • Intellectual pursuits of women
    ○ Gwendolen: "Mamma, whose views on
education are extremely strict, has
brought me up to be extremely short-
sighted; it is part of her system"
    ○ Cecily: "But I don't like German. It
isn't at all a becoming language. I
know perfectly well that I look quite
plain after my German lesson"
  • Female solidarity: Gwendolen and Cecily
eventually stick together "against" the men
  • Class issues
  • Lady Bracknell as caricature of Sarah
Grand

5. How such information influences our understanding
   of Wilde's intentions
   • Exposing Grand's hypocrisy

6. Conclusion
   • Wilde and Grand had very different points
of view
   • Gwendolen and Cecily are disappointing New
Women
   • Wilde uses the play as a vehicle to purposely
offend women like Grand

You would set about writing a formal outline with a similar process,
though in the final stages you would label the headings differently. A
formal outline for a paper that argues the thesis about *The Importance of
Being Earnest* cited above—that Gwendolen and Cecily are Wilde's con-
ceptualizations of Grand's New Woman—might look like this:

Thesis: In *The Importance of Being Earnest*, Oscar Wilde characterizes Cecily and Gwendolen as witty satirizations of the emerging Victorian concept of the New Woman.

I. Introduction and thesis

II. Sarah Grand
    A. Her definitions of the New Woman
        1. She created the "New Woman" label in 1894
        2. She believed that a woman's life should center on civic duty
        3. She was an outspoken critic of the aesthetic movement that Wilde embraced
        4. She disapproved of the public New Woman concept that emerged at the end of the Victorian era
    B. Her ideas
        1. Women should let go of weakness and frivolity that limit true feminine grace and charm
        2. Goals for the New Woman do not include autonomy and self-identity
    C. Her battle with Wilde
        1. Grand openly criticized the aesthetic movement
        2. Wilde and Grand very likely read each other's work

III. Gwendolen and Cecily as examples of the New Woman concept
    A. Gwendolen's immodest flirting and traveling alone: "For women of that era, travel seems to have been the individual gesture of the housebound, male-dominated, very proper lady. . . .

[Traveling,] she could enjoy a freedom of action unthinkable at home. . . . Above all, travel promised a segment of life, a span of time, over which a woman has maximum control" (Holcomb 1)

B. Intellectual pursuits of women

   1. Gwendolen: "Mamma, whose views on education are extremely strict, has brought me up to be extremely short-sighted; it is part of her system"

   2. Cecily: "But I don't like German. It isn't at all a becoming language. I know perfectly well that I look quite plain after my German lesson"

C. Female solidarity: Gwendolen and Cecily eventually stick together "against" the men

D. Class issues/country life versus city life

E. Lady Bracknell as caricature of Sarah Grand

IV. How such information influences our understanding of Wilde's intentions of exposing Grand's hypocrisy

V. Conclusion

A. Gwendolen and Cecily, through their unwitting comic exploits, have provided perfect satirizations of the New Woman. If my connection is true, Wilde has exacted his revenge on the "aesthetic"-loathing Sarah Grand for more than a century.

B. His ability to subtly point out hypocrisy in the context of the Victorian era was impeccable. We will continue to enjoy the exploits and antics of these characters for centuries to come.

As in the previous example outline, the thesis provided the seeds of a structure, and the writer was careful to arrange the supporting points in a logical manner, showing the relationships among the ideas in the paper.

Body Paragraphs

Once your outline is complete, you can begin drafting your paper. Paragraphs, units of related sentences, are the building blocks of a good paper, and as you draft you should keep in mind both the function and the qualities of good paragraphs. Paragraphs help you chart and control the shape and content of your essay, and they help the reader see your organization and your logic. You should begin a new paragraph whenever you move from one major point to another. In longer, more complex essays you might use a group of related paragraphs to support major points. Remember that in addition to being adequately developed, a good paragraph is both unified and coherent.

Unified Paragraphs:

Each paragraph must be centered around one idea or point, and a unified paragraph carefully focuses on and develops this central idea without including extraneous ideas or tangents. For beginning writers, the best way to ensure that you are constructing unified paragraphs is to include a topic sentence in each paragraph. This topic sentence should convey the main point of the paragraph, and every sentence in the paragraph should relate to that topic sentence. Any sentence that strays from the central topic does not belong in the paragraph and needs to be revised or deleted. Consider the following paragraph about christenings in *The Importance of Being Earnest.* Notice how the paragraph veers away from the main point that these christenings are merely machinations to acquire the name Ernest:

> The depiction of women's strength and solidarity continues to crumble in this reconciliation scene. The women discover that Jack and Algernon will undergo the "arduous" task of being christened under the name of Ernest in order to cater to their ideals. Physical strength, often seen as a masculine quality, hardly plays a role in a christening, an act usually reserved for small children. Miss Prism's confession about the handbag alters everyone's lives

considerably, leading us to wonder about issues of child care and the education of women.

Although the paragraph begins solidly, and the first sentence provides the central idea of the paragraph, the author soon goes on a tangent. If the purpose of the paragraph is to demonstrate that the christenings play an integral role in the play, the sentences about the exploits of Miss Prism are tangential here. They may find a place later in the paper, but they should be deleted from this paragraph.

Coherent Paragraphs:

In addition to shaping unified paragraphs, you must also craft coherent paragraphs, paragraphs that develop their points logically with sentences that flow smoothly into one another. Coherence depends on the order of your sentences, but it is not strictly the order of the sentences that is important to paragraph coherence. You also need to craft your prose to help the reader see the relationship among the sentences.

Consider the following paragraph about christenings in *The Importance of Being Earnest*. Notice how the writer uses the same ideas as the paragraph above yet fails to help the reader see the relationships among the points.

The women discover that Jack and Algernon will undergo the "arduous" task of being christened under the name of Ernest in order to cater to their ideals. Gwendolen exclaims passionately, "How absurd to talk of the equality of the sexes! Where questions of self-sacrifice are concerned, men are infinitely beyond us." Cecily says, "They have moments of physical courage of which we women know absolutely nothing" (2,213). Jack, readily puffed up with pride, agrees with both of the women while clasping hands with Algernon. Ironically, this depiction of derisory solidarity between the two men is an inversion of what occurred between the women a few minutes ago.

This paragraph demonstrates that unity alone does not guarantee paragraph effectiveness. The argument is hard to follow because the author fails both to show connections between the sentences and to indicate how they work to support the overall point.

A number of techniques are available to aid paragraph coherence. Careful use of transitional words and phrases is essential. You can use transitional flags to introduce an example or an illustration *(for example, for instance)*, to amplify a point or add another phase of the same idea *(additionally, furthermore, next, similarly, finally, then)*, to indicate a conclusion or result *(therefore, as a result, thus, in other words)*, to signal a contrast or a qualification *(on the other hand, nevertheless, despite this, on the contrary, still, however, conversely)*, to signal a comparison *(likewise, in comparison, similarly)*, and to indicate a movement in time *(afterward, earlier, eventually, finally, later, subsequently, until)*.

In addition to transitional flags, careful use of pronouns aids coherence and flow. If you were writing about *The Wizard of Oz*, you would not want to keep repeating the phrase *the witch* or the name *Dorothy*. Careful substitution of the pronoun *she* in these instances can aid coherence. A word of warning, though: When you substitute pronouns for proper names, always be sure that your pronoun reference is clear. In a paragraph that discusses both Dorothy and the witch, substituting *she* could lead to confusion. Make sure that it is clear to whom the pronoun refers. Generally, the pronoun refers to the last proper noun you have used.

While repeating the same name over and over again can lead to awkward, boring prose, it is possible to use repetition to help your paragraph's coherence. Careful repetition of important words or phrases can lend coherence to your paragraph by reminding readers of your key points. Admittedly, it takes some practice to use this technique effectively. You may find that reading your prose aloud can help you develop an ear for effective use of repetition.

To see how helpful transitional aids are, compare the paragraph below to the preceding paragraph about christenings in *The Importance of Being Earnest*. Notice how the author works with the same ideas and quotations but shapes them into a much more coherent paragraph whose point is clearer and easier to follow.

> The depiction of women's strength and solidarity continues to crumble in this reconciliation scene. The women discover that Jack and Algernon will undergo the "arduous" task of being christened under the name of

Ernest in order to cater to their ideals. They immediately resort to criticizing the female gender, who would never consider such a courageous act. Gwendolen exclaims passionately, "How absurd to talk of the equality of the sexes! Where questions of self-sacrifice are concerned, men are infinitely beyond us." Cecily seconds this by saying, "They have moments of physical courage of which we women know absolutely nothing" (2,213). Physical strength, often seen as a masculine quality, hardly plays a role in a christening, an act usually reserved for small children. Jack, readily puffed up with pride, agrees with both of the women while clasping hands with Algernon. Ironically, this depiction of derisory solidarity between the two men is an inversion of what occurred between the women a few minutes ago.

Similarly, the following paragraph demonstrates both unity and coherence. In it, the author argues that Gwendolen's travel habits reveal her status as a New Woman of sorts.

Traveling remains an important aspect of the play, as the characters move locations from the city to Jack's estate in the countryside. The character of Gwendolen travels without an escort, something that would have been seen as a huge "breach of Victorian convention" (Holcomb 2). Many New Women used travel to foreign countries as a method of escaping the patriarchal restrictions that plagued them in their homelands. As foreigners they were not held to gender restrictions present in their destinations:

For women of that era, travel seems to have been the individual gesture of the housebound, male-dominated, very proper lady, . . . [Traveling.] she could enjoy a freedom of action unthinkable at home. . . . Above all, travel promised a segment of life, a span of time, over which a woman has maximum control. (Holcomb 1)

Indeed, Gwendolen invades Jack's countryside estate as a whirling dervish of energy and demand. Finally free from the restraints of her mother and possible scandal, she hunts down her true love, Ernest, with a restless zeal. This journey from her environment to another is not an act of "self discovery" but one designed to secure a state of matrimony (Holcomb 2). Unlike other "young female Victorian eyes peering out from windows forced shut against a tempting world," Gwendolen appears oblivious to everything save for Jack (2).

Introductions

Introductions present particular challenges for writers. Generally, your introduction should do two things: capture your reader's attention and explain the main point of your essay. In other words, while your introduction should contain your thesis, it needs to do a bit more work than that. You are likely to find that starting that first paragraph is one of the most difficult parts of the paper. It is hard to face that blank page or screen, and as a result, many beginning writers, in desperation to start somewhere, start with overly broad, general statements. While it is often a good strategy to start with more general subject matter and narrow your focus, do not begin with broad sweeping statements such as Everyone likes to be creative and feel understood. Such sentences are nothing but empty filler. They begin to fill the blank page, but they do nothing to advance your argument. Instead, you should try to gain your readers' interest. Some writers like to begin with a pertinent quotation or with a relevant question. Or you might begin with an introduction of the topic you will discuss. If you are writing about Wilde's presentation of the New Woman during the late 19th century in *The Importance of Being Earnest,* for instance, you might begin by talking about definitions of the New Woman. Another common trap to avoid is depending on your title to introduce the author and the text you are writing about. Always include the work's author and title in your opening paragraph.

Compare the effectiveness of the following introductions.

1.   Throughout history, women have been oppressed. Think how you feel when you really want something: It makes you feel bad when you don't get it, right?

In this story, Wilde shows characters' different points of view about women. More importantly, he shows how New Women function.

2. Oscar Wilde remains one of the savviest social commentators to ever have existed. His ability to critique the Victorian upper class's double standards while still drawing in the audience with his humor makes him a master of comedic staging. Not a single institution, including religion and marriage, was considered sacred or protected from his jabs. He would also find a wealth of hypocrisy with some of the feminists who championed the cause of the "New Woman." *The Importance of Being Earnest* provides a perfect battleground for such a subject. The characters of Cecily and Gwendolen in Wilde's comedic masterpiece are witty satirizations of this emerging concept of the Victorian era.

  Conflicting definitions of the New Woman have existed since the idea first appeared at the turn of the 20th century. In modern times, we tend to think of the New Woman as someone who fled the domestic sphere, embraced her sexuality, rejected the idea of marriage, and completely abandoned all other social conventions applied to the female sex. There was some truth to this concept, as women were first able to enter the professional working world at this time. They were often able to earn money, thus gaining some autonomy from their parents. The idea of a dating scene opened up, as inexpensive amusements became more available. However, although they experienced a few years of independence, the vast majority of women returned to the world of their mothers and the inevitable matrimony it implied (Ohio State University 1).

The first introduction begins with a vague, overly broad sentence; cites unclear, undeveloped examples; and then moves abruptly to the very weak thesis. Notice, too, how a reader deprived of the paper's title does not know the name of the work that the paper will analyze. The second introduction uses the same material and thesis but provides more detail and is consequently much more interesting. It begins by discussing Oscar Wilde's reputation and tactics as a social writer, briefly mentions definitions of the New Woman, and then gives specific examples that fit this definition. The paragraph ends with the thesis. This effective introduction also includes the title of the text and full name of the author.

The paragraph below provides another example of an opening strategy. It begins by introducing the author and the text it will analyze, and then it moves on by briefly introducing relevant details of the story in order to set up its thesis.

> Oscar Wilde's play *The Importance of Being Earnest* centers on Gwendolen and Cecily, two female characters doing their best to marry men named Ernest. Wilde's ideas about the New Woman of the late Victorian era come through rather unexpectedly, since most readers do not consider Gwendolen and Cecily as models of strong independent women. What Wilde does in this play is use Gwendolen and Cecily as vehicles for satirizing a particular concept of the New Woman, promoted by Sarah Grand, an outspoken critic of Wilde's own aesthetic movement.

Conclusions

Conclusions present another series of challenges for writers. No doubt you have heard the old adage about writing papers: "Tell us what you are going to say, say it, and then tell us what you've said." While this formula does not necessarily result in bad papers, it does not often result in good ones either. It will almost certainly result in boring papers (especially boring conclusions). If you have done a good job establishing your points in the body of the paper, the reader already knows and understands your argument. There is no need to merely reiterate. Do not just summarize your main points in your conclusion. Such a boring and mechanical conclusion does nothing to advance your argument or interest your reader. Consider the following conclusion to a paper about the New Woman in *The Importance of Being Earnest.*

> In conclusion, Wilde uses the concept of the New Woman in
> his play. Gwendolen and Cecily are examples. Wilde pokes
> fun at some interpretations of the New Woman through his
> characterizations. We should all remember that.

Besides starting with a mechanical transitional device, this conclusion
does little more than summarize the main points of the outline (and it
does not even touch on all of them). It is incomplete and uninteresting
(and a little too depressing).

Instead, your conclusion should add something to your paper. A good
tactic is to build on the points you have been arguing. Asking "why?"
often helps you draw further conclusions. For example, in an essay on
The Importance of Being Earnest, you might speculate or explain how the
concept of the New Woman speaks to how Wilde presents female characters in the play in order to convey his beliefs about right and wrong ways
to promote gender equality. Another method of successfully concluding
an essay is to speculate on other directions in which to take your topic
by tying it to larger issues. You might do this by envisioning your paper
as just one section of a larger paper. Having established your points in
this paper, how would you build on this argument? Where would you go
next? In the following conclusion to a paper on *The Importance of Being
Earnest,* the author reiterates some of the main points of the paper but
does so in order to amplify the discussion of the play's central message
and to connect it to the historical context of Oscar Wilde's work:

> Gwendolen and Cecily, through their unwitting comic
> exploits, have provided perfect satirizations of the
> New Woman. If my connection is true, Wilde has exacted
> his revenge on the "aesthetic"-loathing Sarah Grand
> for more than a century. His ability to subtly point
> out hypocrisy in the context of the Victorian era was
> impeccable. We will continue to enjoy the exploits and
> antics of these characters for centuries to come.

Citations and Formatting

Using Primary Sources:

As the examples included in this chapter indicate, strong papers on literary texts incorporate quotations from the text in order to support their

points. It is not enough for you to assert your interpretation without providing support or evidence from the text. Without well-chosen quotations to support your argument you are, in effect, saying to the reader, "Take my word for it." It is important to use quotations thoughtfully and selectively. Remember that the paper presents *your* argument, so choose quotations that support *your* assertions. Do not let the author's voice overwhelm your own. With that caution in mind, there are some guidelines you should follow to ensure that you use quotations clearly and effectively.

Integrate Quotations:

Quotations should always be integrated into your own prose. Do not just drop them into your paper without introduction or comment. Otherwise, it is unlikely that your reader will see their function. You can integrate textual support easily and clearly with identifying tags, short phrases that identify the speaker. For example:

> Jack responds, "Oh, pleasure, pleasure!"

While this tag appears before the quotation, you can also use tags after or in the middle of the quoted text, as the following examples demonstrate:

> "What else should bring one anywhere?" asks Jack.

> "I have only been married once," Lane tells Algernon. "That was in consequence of a misunderstanding between myself and a young person."

You can also use a colon to formally introduce a quotation:

> It is clear that Algernon takes offense: "I believe it is customary in good society to take some slight refreshment at five o'clock."

When you quote brief sections of poems (three lines or fewer), use slash marks to indicate the line breaks in the poem:

As the poem ends, Dickinson speaks of the power of the imagination: "The revery alone will do, / If bees are few."

Longer quotations (more than four lines of prose or three lines of poetry) should be set off from the rest of your paper in a block quotation. Double-space before you begin the passage, indent it 10 spaces from your left-hand margin, and double-space the passage itself. Because the indentation signals the inclusion of a quotation, do not use quotation marks around the cited passage. Use a colon to introduce the passage, as in the following two examples:

Algernon has clear views on marriage at the beginning of the play:

> I really don't see anything romantic in proposing. It is very romantic to be in love. But there is nothing romantic about a definite proposal. Why, one may be accepted. One usually is, I believe. Then the excitement is all over. The very essence of romance is uncertainty. If ever I get married, I'll certainly try to forget the fact.

Clearly, Algernon regards himself as a confirmed bachelor.

The whole of Dickinson's poem speaks of the imagination:

> To make a prairie it takes a clover and
>   one bee,
> One clover, and a bee,
> And revery.
> The revery alone will do,
> If bees are few.

Clearly, she argues for the creative power of the mind.

It is also important to interpret quotations after you introduce them and explain how they help advance your point. You cannot assume that your reader will interpret the quotations the same way that you do.

Quote Accurately:
Always quote accurately. Anything within quotations marks must be the author's exact words. There are, however, some rules to follow if you need to modify the quotation to fit into your prose.

1. Use brackets to indicate any material that might have been added to the author's exact wording. For example, if you need to add any words to the quotation or alter it grammatically to allow it to fit into your prose, indicate your changes in brackets:

   ```
   Jack counters Algernon's suggestion by stating,
   "There is no good offering a reward now that
   the [cigarette case] is found."
   ```

2. Conversely, if you choose to omit any words from the quotation, use ellipses (three spaced periods) to indicate missing words or phrases:

   ```
   Jack tells Algernon, "I have been writing frantic
   letters . . . about it."
   ```

3. If you delete a sentence or more, use the ellipses after a period:

   ```
   Algernon defends himself to Jack: "It isn't. . . .
   It accounts for the extraordinary number of
   bachelors that one sees all over the place."
   ```

4. If you omit a line or more of poetry, or more than one paragraph of prose, use a single line of spaced periods to indicate the omission:

   ```
   To make a prairie it takes a clover and
   one bee,
   . . . . . . . . . . . . . . . .
   And revery.
   ```

```
The revery alone will do,
If bees are few.
```

Punctuate Properly:

Punctuation of quotations often causes more trouble than it should. Once again, you just need to keep these simple rules in mind.

1. Periods and commas should be placed inside quotation marks, even if they are not part of the original quotation:

   ```
   Jack admits the truth to Lady Bracknell: "I have
   lost both my parents."
   ```

   The only exception to this rule is when the quotation is followed by a parenthetical reference. In this case, the period or comma goes after the citation (more on these later in this chapter):

   ```
   Jack admits the truth to Lady Bracknell: "I have
   lost both my parents" (2,189).
   ```

2. Other marks of punctuation—colons, semicolons, question marks, and exclamation points—go outside the quotation marks unless they are part of the original quotation:

   ```
   Why does Lady Bracknell tell Jack that "to lose
   both seems like carelessness"?
   ```

Documenting Primary Sources:

Unless you are instructed otherwise, you should provide sufficient information for your reader to locate material you quote. Generally, literature papers follow the rules set forth by the Modern Language Association (MLA). These can be found in the *MLA Handbook for Writers of Research Papers* (sixth edition). You should be able to find this book in the reference section of your library. Additionally, its rules for citing both primary and secondary sources are widely available from reputable online sources. One of these is the Online Writing Lab (OWL) at Purdue University. OWL's guide to MLA style is available at http://owl.english.purdue.edu/owl/resource/557/01/.

The Modern Language Association also offers answers to frequently asked questions about MLA style on this helpful Web page: http://www.mla.org/style_faq. Generally, when you are citing from literary works in papers, you should keep a few guidelines in mind.

Parenthetical Citations:

MLA asks for parenthetical references in your text after quotations. When you are working with prose (short stories, novels, or essays) include page numbers in the parentheses:

> Algernon defends himself to Jack: "It isn't. . . . It accounts for the extraordinary number of bachelors that one sees all over the place" (2,180).

When you are quoting poetry, include line numbers:

> Dickinson's speaker tells of the arrival of a fly: "There interposed a Fly -- / With Blue -- uncertain stumbling Buzz -- / Between the light -- and Me -- " (12–14).

Works Cited Page:

These parenthetical citations are linked to a separate works cited page at the end of the paper. The works cited page lists works alphabetically by the authors' last name. An entry for the above reference to Wilde's *The Importance of Being Earnest* would read:

> Wilde, Oscar. *The Importance of Being Earnest. The Norton Anthology: English Literature.* Eds. M. H. Abrams and Stephen Greenblatt. New York: W. W. Norton and Co., 2001. 2,177–223.

The *MLA Handbook* includes a full listing of sample entries, as do many of the online explanations of MLA style.

Documenting Secondary Sources:

To ensure that your paper is built entirely upon your own ideas and analysis, instructors often ask that you write interpretative papers without any outside research. If, on the other hand, your paper requires research, you must document any secondary sources you use. You need to document direct quotations, summaries or paraphrases of others' ideas, and factual information that is not common knowledge. Follow the guidelines above for quoting primary sources when you use direct quotations from secondary sources. Keep in mind that MLA style also includes specific guidelines for citing electronic sources. OWL's Web site provides a good summary: http://owl.english.purdue.edu/owl/resource/557/09/.

Parenthetical Citations:

As with the documentation of primary sources, described above, MLA guidelines require in-text parenthetical references to your secondary sources. Unlike the research papers you might write for a history class, literary research papers following MLA style do not use footnotes as a means of documenting sources. Instead, after a quotation, you should cite the author's last name and the page number:

> Jack admits the truth to Lady Bracknell: "I have lost both my parents" (Wilde 2,189).

If you include the name of the author in your prose, then you would include only the page number in your citation. For example:

> Clearly Wilde intends for Algernon to take offense: "I believe it is customary in good society to take some slight refreshment at five o'clock" (2,179).

If you are including more than one work by the same author, the parenthetical citation should include a shortened yet identifiable version of the title in order to indicate which of the author's works you cite. For example:

> Clearly Wilde intends for Algernon to take offense: "I believe it is customary in good society to take some slight refreshment at five o'clock" (*Importance* 2,179).

Similarly, and just as important, if you summarize or paraphrase the particular ideas of your source, you must provide documentation:

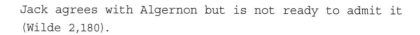

Jack agrees with Algernon but is not ready to admit it (Wilde 2,180).

Works Cited Page:

Like the primary sources discussed above, the parenthetical references to secondary sources are keyed to a separate works cited page at the end of your paper. Here is an example of a works cited page that uses the examples cited above. Note that when two or more works by the same author are listed, you should use three hyphens followed by a period in the subsequent entries. You can find a complete list of sample entries in the *MLA Handbook* or from a reputable online summary of MLA style.

WORKS CITED

Holcomb, Briavel. "Women Travellers at Fins de Siecles." *Focus* 43.4 (Winter 1993): 11-15. Academic Search Premier. 23 Apr 2006.

"The New Woman." *Clash of Cultures*. 2005. Ohio State University History Department. 23 Apr. 2006.

Parker, Oliver, dir. *The Importance of Being Earnest*. Miramax, 2002.

Richardson, Angelique. "The Eugenization of Love: Sarah Grand and the Morality of Genealogy." *Victorian Studies* 42:2 (Winter 1999–2000): 227-55.

Wilde, Oscar. *The Importance of Being Earnest*. *The Norton Anthology: English Literature*. Eds. M. H. Abrams and Stephen Greenblatt. New York: W. W. Norton, 2001. 2,177-223.

Plagiarism:

Failure to document carefully and thoroughly can leave you open to charges of stealing the ideas of others, which is known as plagiarism, and this is a very serious matter. Remember that it is important to include quotation marks when you use language from your source, even if you use just one or two words. For example, if you wrote, Algernon believes it is customary in good society, you would be guilty of plagiarism, since you used Wilde's distinct language without acknowledging him as the source. Instead, you should write: Algernon says that "it is customary in good society to take some slight refreshment at five o'clock" (Wilde 2,179). In this case, you have properly credited Wilde.

Similarly, neither summarizing the ideas of an author nor changing or omitting just a few words means that you can omit a citation. Vyvyan Holland's book *Son of Oscar Wilde* contains the following passage:

> Most small boys adore their fathers, and we adored ours; and as all good fathers are, he was a hero to us both. . . . There was nothing about him of the monster that some people who never knew him and never even saw him have tried to make him out to be. He was a real companion to us, and we always looked forward eagerly to his frequent visits to our nursery. Most parents in those days were far too solemn and pompous with their children, insisting on a vast amount of usually undeserved respect. My own father was quite different; he had so much of the child in his own nature that he delighted in playing our games. (Holland 52)

Below are two examples of plagiarized passages:

> Vyvyan Holland loved his father and, like a lot of kids, really looked up to him. He did not know the vicious person that many people believed Wilde to be. All he knew was that his father was not serious and overly inflated like many parents.

> Holland contends that his father was quite different, especially given the fact that he was very much a child in his own nature (Holland 52).

While the first passage does not use Holland's exact language, it does list some of the same examples as the book. Since this interpretation is Holland's distinct idea, this constitutes plagiarism. The second passage has shortened his passage, changed some wording, and included a citation, but some of the phrasing is Holland's. The first passage could be fixed with a parenthetical citation. Because some of the wording in the second remains the same, though, it would require the use of quotation marks, in addition to a parenthetical citation. The passage below represents an honestly and adequately documented use of the original passage:

Vyvyan Holland remembers his childhood very fondly: "Most small boys adore their fathers, and we adored ours; and as all good fathers are, he was a hero to us both . . . There was nothing about him of the monster that some people who never knew him and never even saw him have tried to make him out to be" (52).

This passage acknowledges that the interpretation is derived from Holland while appropriately using quotations to indicate his precise language.

While it is not necessary to document well-known facts, often referred to as "common knowledge," any ideas or language that you take from someone else must be properly documented. Common knowledge generally includes the birth and death dates of authors or other well-documented facts of their lives. An often-cited guideline is that if you can find the information in three sources, it is common knowledge. Despite this guideline, it is, admittedly, often difficult to know if the facts you uncover are common knowledge or not. When in doubt, document your source.

Sample Essay

Andrea Schmidt
Dr. Watkin
Victorian Literature
February 22, 2010

THE IMPORTANCE OF THE NEW WOMAN

Oscar Wilde remains one of the savviest social commentators to ever have existed. His ability to critique the Victorian upper class's double standards while still drawing in the audience with his humor makes him a master of comedic staging. Not a single institution, including religion and marriage, was considered sacred or protected from his jabs. He would also find a wealth of hypocrisy with some of the feminists who championed the cause of the "New Woman." *The Importance of Being Earnest* provides a perfect battleground for such a subject. The characters of Cecily and Gwendolen in Wilde's comedic masterpiece are witty satirizations of this emerging concept of the Victorian era.

Conflicting definitions of the New Woman have existed since the idea first appeared at the turn of the 20th century. In modern times, we tend to think of the New Woman as someone who fled the domestic sphere, embraced her sexuality, rejected the idea of marriage, and completely abandoned all other social conventions applied to the female sex. There was some truth to this concept, as women were first able to enter the professional working world at this time. They were often able to earn money, thus gaining some autonomy from their parents. The idea of a dating scene opened up, as inexpensive amusements became more available. However, although they experienced a few years of independence, the vast majority of women returned to the world of their mothers and the matrimony it implied (Ohio State University 1).

It appears that the New Woman concept originated as something even tamer. Sarah Grand, a writer and social advocate, claims to have created the label of the New Woman in 1894. Grand believed that a woman's life should be geared toward the fulfillment of all of her civic duties (Richardson 227). Thus, women should let go of the weaknesses and frivolities that limit their true feminine grace and charm. The goals of the New Woman, according to Grand, were not to seek autonomy and self-identity but rather to seek a better way to improve the domestic sphere and serve men (228). However, as time passed, Grand became disenchanted with the way in which the idea was being shaped and formed, viewing the New Woman that later emerged as a "vulgar creature" (228).

I would like to suggest that Oscar Wilde uses his characters in *The Importance of Being Earnest* to satirize specifically Grand's concept of the New Woman.

Grand was an open critic of the aesthetic movement. She believed that the artist had a social obligation to civic and moral duties, not to merely create art for art's sake (Richardson 241). Oscar Wilde, a decadent and also a well-known public figure, was an avid supporter and participant in such a movement. I would find it absurd if Grand had not been aware of Wilde's work, and the "moral" scandals he was involved in most likely would have appalled her. Although we as modern-day readers cannot go back in time and ask him directly, I would not find it surprising that Wilde was aware of the highly vocal social activist's work and commentary. It is safe to say that he would find plenty to satirize in Grand's concept of the New Woman and her horror at its evolution.

In the first act of the play, Algernon states to his love-struck friend, "Girls never marry the men they flirt with. Girls don't think it is right" (Wilde 2,180). Gwendolen behaves in a very flirtatious manner with Jack in comparison to the socially expected modest behavior usually accorded to young ladies. Women during this time period first began to date or develop romantic relations with more than just one man. Gwendolen foregoes a traditional courtship and rebels instead against the wishes of her mother. She attempts to assert her independence and autonomy from Lady Bracknell, but she does this in pursuit of a domestic situation with Jack.

Traveling remains an important aspect of the play, as the characters move locations from the city to Jack's estate in the countryside. The character of Gwendolen travels without an escort, something that would have been seen as a huge "breach of Victorian convention" (Holcomb 2). Many New Women used travel to foreign countries as a method of escaping the patriarchal restrictions that plagued them in their homelands. As foreigners they were not held to gender restrictions present in their destinations:

> For women of that era, travel seems to have been
> the individual gesture of the housebound, male-
> dominated, very proper lady. . . . [Traveling,]
> she could enjoy a freedom of action unthinkable at
> home. . . . Above all, travel promised a segment
> of life, a span of time, over which a woman has
> maximum control. (Holcomb 1)

Indeed, Gwendolen invades Jack's countryside estate as a whirling dervish of energy and demand. Finally free of the restraints of her mother and possible scandal, she hunts down her true love, Ernest, with a restless zeal. This journey from her usual environment to another is not an act of "self discovery" but one designed to secure a state of matrimony (Holcomb 2). Unlike other "young female Victorian eyes peering out from windows forced shut against a tempting world," Gwendolen appears oblivious to everything save for Jack (2).

Intellectual pursuits were seen as a method for the New Woman to improve herself and gain a greater foothold within the civic world (Ohio State University 1). It is obvious through his writings that Wilde saw the education of a woman as not a pursuit of particular worth. Neither Gwendolen nor Cecily appear to possess any great intellect, although not much can be said for any of the other characters either.

Gwendolen swiftly informs Cecily that "Mamma, whose views on education are extremely strict, has brought me up to be extremely shortsighted; it is part of her system" (Wilde 2,206). The fact that she has never been allowed to actively pursue an education leaves her in a state of powerlessness that makes it easy for her mother to control her. However, this does not seem to bother her very much, as she does not pursue any intellectual studies throughout the play, aside from the reading of her own "sensational" diary on the train (2,206). Even though Gwendolen likes to think of herself as naturally intelligent, the results are almost laughable. When she first meets Cecily, Gwendolen informs her of her uncanny abilities: "Something tells me that we are going to be great friends. I like you already more than I can say. My first impressions of people are never wrong" (2,205). However, Gwendolen's shortsightedness immediately comes into play when she exclaims to Cecily moments later: "From the moment I saw you I distrusted you. I felt that you were false and deceitful. I am never deceived in such matters. My first impressions of people are invariably right" (2,209). Wilde also uses the characters of Cecily and Miss Prism to satirize the educational pursuits of women. He depicts Cecily as an extremely inattentive, rather shallow pupil. When Miss Prism suggests that she return to her studies, Cecily replies, "But I don't like German. It isn't at all a becoming language. I know perfectly well that I look quite plain after my German lesson." She absurdly identifies her education as something that hinders her feminine attractiveness, a quality deemed important during this era. She pursues "utilitarian," domestic pursuits such as watering flowers instead of following Jack's wishes of improving herself "in every way" as much as possible (2,194). She even states to Algernon that she would not care to be in love with a sensible man, because she "shouldn't know what to talk to him about" (2,198). This implies that she can only enjoy shallow, meaningless conversations.

Cecily counters the opinions of New Women such as Gertrude Bell, who rebelled against the trivial pursuits considered suitable for a women's education, stating, "I'm so consumably bored . . . I want to know one thing in the world well at least. I'm tired of learning in this dilettante way" (Holcomb 2). Bell probably would have jumped at the chance to study a subject such as German and have found it laughable that Cecily finds it so boring.

The hope of the New Woman was also to be free of all of the labels and constraints normally associated with social class. During the 1890s, a character known as the "Gibson girl" remained a prominent symbol for the New Woman. Her clothes did not give any hint as to her social standing. She transcended anything that would situate her in a hierarchy while she went in pursuit of activities and accomplishments (Ohio State University 1).

However, the power associated with class continues to remain very important to Gwendolen and Cecily, as is evident in their initial meeting. Without any hesitance, Gwendolen feels it necessary to tell Cecily of her patriarchal lineage. Then, in an effort to degrade the woman whom she believes to be her romantic rival, Gwendolen undertakes an absurd, relentless effort to put Cecily in her place. She comically informs Cecily that her below-par offerings of cake and sugar are "rarely seen in the best houses nowadays" and are "not fashionable anymore" (2,208). Cecily retaliates domestically by serving exactly such a spread. Gwendolen bristles with anger and warns her that she "goes too far" (2,208). A perpetual battle of town versus country ensues. Gwendolen looks down on the countryside as being reserved for rough, agricultural labor: "I am glad to say that I have never seen a spade. It is obvious that our social spheres have been widely different" (2,207). Cecily is quick to point out her hypocrisy in hating the feelings of being crowded (2,208). Blindness to class and social standing appears a far-off dream in this scene.

The New Woman was also expected to form a sort of solidarity with other women who shared her same sort of beliefs and ideals. When Cecily and Gwendolen find that Jack and Algernon have deceived them, they immediately form a pact made comical by its absurd immediacy:

GWENDOLEN: My poor wounded Cecily!
CECILY: My sweet wronged Gwendolen!

GWENDOLEN: You will call me sister will you not?
(2,209)

The strength of this pact remains highly dubious, as moments before they had loathed and threatened each other.

It appears even more ironic when the women retreat into the house, the domestic sphere they are inevitably expected to inhabit. Gwendolen states with assurance, "[Jack and Algernon] will hardly venture to come after us there" (2,210). Although they stand up to these two men who have manipulated and lied to them, they immediately return to the only place considered suitable for women: the home.

Their front of solidarity quickly falls apart when the men approach, leaving great doubt as to the strength of the women's independence. Although determined that they shall not be the first to speak, Gwendolen quickly blurts out a question. The young women are taken away with the aesthetics of the replies rather than with the evidence behind their explanations. Gwendolen states, "In matters of grave importance, style, not sincerity is the vital thing" (2,212). The "important principles at stake" amount to nothing more than a changing of their names to that of Ernest (2,213).

The depiction of women's strength and solidarity continues to crumble in this reconciliation scene. The women discover that Jack and Algernon will undergo the "arduous" task of being christened under the name of Ernest in order to cater to their ideals. They immediately resort to criticizing the female gender, who would never consider such a courageous act. Gwendolen exclaims passionately, "How absurd to talk of the equality of the sexes! Where questions of self-sacrifice are concerned, men are infinitely beyond us." Cecily seconds this by saying, "They have moments of physical courage of which we women know absolutely nothing" (2,213). Physical strength, often seen as a masculine quality, hardly plays a role in a christening, an act usually reserved for small children. Jack, readily puffed up with pride, agrees with both of the women while clasping hands with Algernon. Ironically, this depiction of derisory solidarity between the two men is an inversion of what occurred between the women a few minutes ago.

It is also humorous that both Cecily and Gwendolen remain fixed on the concept of the name Ernest. They are greatly upset when they find out their respective lovers do not possess the name. This harkens back to women's required search for a patriarchal name, through marriage, that would give them power and self-identity. Initially, neither of them feel they could marry a man who did not have the name. Gwendolen chides her lover that "Jack is a notorious domesticity for John! The only really safe name is Ernest" (2,187).

When it appears inevitable that Cecily and Algernon will marry, Miss Prism resigns from her post as a tutor, stating that she can give her no further instruction as she has surpassed her in her education by finding someone to marry (Parker 2002). All of her instruction and lecturing on the importance of Cecily continuing her studies has been undermined, for Miss Prism believes that the state of matrimony is the highest ideal women can strive for. With the onset of marriage, all forms of improving her intellect must stop, for there remains no other way upon which she could elevate herself. Wilde gleefully satirizes the fact that the New Woman was expected to improve her mind but only so she could have intelligent conversations with her husband.

On a whole, Lady Bracknell remains the harshest critic of these two young women. She censures Gwendolen because Gwendolen wishes to flee the domestic sphere of her mother for Jack. Instead, Lady Bracknell demands that Gwendolen marry a man who surpasses her in social power and wealth. She zealously interrogates Jack about his history and obsessively tracks down her daughter when she goes missing. Hypocritically, Lady Bracknell admits that when she married Lord Bracknell, she "had no fortune of any kind" but did not allow that to "stand in [her] way" (2,216).

It is also ironic that Lady Bracknell seems to be the dominant party in the relationship with her husband. We hear often of Lord Bracknell, but he never appears in the play, and it seems that Lady Bracknell has no connection to him other than his name. Gwendolen's description of her father gives insight as to how he is treated in the home.

> Outside the family circle, papa, I am glad to say, is entirely unknown. I think that it quite as it should be. The home seems to me the proper sphere for the man. And certainly once a man begins to neglect his domestic duties he becomes painfully effeminate, does he not? (2,205)

It appears that while Lady Bracknell revels in going about in the world, she has consigned her husband to the environment usually reserved for women, the home. I would go so far as to say that Lady Bracknell could be viewed as a caricature of Sarah Grand, a woman who often took hypocritical stances in regard to the New Woman.

Gwendolen and Cecily, through their unwitting comic exploits, have provided perfect satirizations of the New Woman. If my connection is true, Wilde has exacted his revenge on the "aesthetic"-loathing Sarah Grand for more than a century. His ability to subtly point out hypocrisy in the context of the Victorian era impeccable. We will continue to enjoy the exploits and antics of these characters for centuries to come.

WORKS CITED

Holcomb, Briavel. "Women Travellers at Fins de Siecles." *Focus* 43.4 (Winter 1993): 11–15. Academic Search Premier. 23 Apr. 2006.

"The New Woman." *Clash of Cultures.* 2005. Ohio State
University History Department. 23 Apr. 2006.

Parker, Oliver, dir. *The Importance of Being Earnest.*
Miramax, 2002.

Richardson, Angelique. "The Eugenization of Love: Sarah
Grand and the Morality of Genealogy." *Victorian
Studies* 42:2 (Winter 1999–2000): 227–55.

Wilde, Oscar. *The Importance of Being Earnest. The Norton
Anthology: English Literature.* Eds. M. H. Abrams and
Stephen Greenblatt. New York: W. W. Norton and Co.,
2001. 2,177–223.

HOW TO WRITE ABOUT
OSCAR WILDE

HIS LEGACY

WILDE'S LEGACY is complicated, to say the least. He left his mark as a student, personality, husband, friend, father, lover, essayist, dandy, prisoner, Irishman, Englishman, "Playwright, Essayist, Novelist, Poet, Epigrammatist, Fashion Czar, Lord of High Society, and Idiosyncratic Socialist" (Nunokawa 2). At the same time, his legacy is quite simple. He was kind, generous, and thoughtful. He was a genius. He was a brilliant conversationalist. He was witty. He was a celebrity. He was Wilde.

The saying goes that if you hear a famous saying and it did not come from the Bible, chances are it was spoken or written by William Shakespeare, George Bernard Shaw, or Oscar Wilde. In 1954 Wilde's grandson, Merlin Holland, claimed that "More books have been written, in more languages, about Oscar Wilde than about any literary figure who has lived during the past hundred years" (198). Whether or not this fact is still true, it is clear that Wilde is an important figure in the world of literature.

Wilde's relatively recent (late 20th-century) fame has stemmed largely from scholars' and fans' focus on his homosexuality. The Oscar Wilde Bookshop in New York City opened in 1967 and at the time was the only "gay bookstore" in the world (Newman xiii); it closed in 2009. There are lip prints covering his tombstone in Paris, left by devoted readers and followers and many who admire Wilde for his courage to come out of the closet during a time when doing so was quite literally against the law. Wilde, however, may never have intended to be a martyr for sexual orientation issues. He was already cast aside for many other reasons:

> He was ostracized and forced into exile by the guardians of tradition, cast by the liberals in the role of the martyred artist, victimized by puritan prides and Pharisees, dismissed by literary historians as a brilliant epigon caught between the Victorian Age and modern times, and smugly classified by the critics as a first-class representative of the second division. And yet his works are always in print, his books are bought and read, and his plays are continually being produced. (Kohl 1)

It is difficult to separate Wilde's life from his work. In fact, it is difficult to even figure out whether or not such a separation is even necessary: "in the one instance, his writings are used to illuminate the personality of the author, and in the second the personality is regarded as the key to understanding the work" (Kohl 2). An overlap between Wilde's life and work seems inescapable. As Norbert Kohl writes, overemphasizing Wilde's life leads to (or comes from) a view of his work as insincere, or one giant memoir. It is, therefore, very interesting to read works on Wilde written through the years to see points of view of those who actually knew him and to see changes in society (i.e., attitudes toward homosexuality) that have influenced how we read, regard, and think about Wilde. It is even more fun to read books about Wilde when you consider what Wilde himself wrote about the practice: "Every great man nowadays has his disciple, and it is always Judas who writes the biography" (Wilde, *Critic as Artist* 1,010).

Wilde knew his talents at speaking, and relished opportunities to use his wit and leave a crowd speechless: "Wilde, clever at duping the makers of worldly celebrity, knew how to project, beyond his real character, an amusing phantom which he played most spiritedly" (Gide 1). Scholars have spent a lot of time figuring out which Wilde was the true Wilde: "Of his wisdom or indeed of his folly, he uttered only what he believed his hearer would relish; he served each, according to his appetite, his taste; those who expected nothing of him had nothing, or just a bit of light froth; and as his first concern was to amuse, many of those who thought they knew him knew only the jester in him" (Gide 2).

Many of the biographies and other works about Wilde were written by people who actually knew him. Interestingly, these writers do not always agree on facets of Wilde's personality, making it clear that Wilde projected particular pieces of himself in various situations, and that perhaps no one fully knew or understood the real man.

Wilde was born in Ireland in 1854. His mother, Jane Francesca Elgee (later Lady Wilde), and his father, William Wilde, were larger-than-life figures in Wilde's life, as parents, as lovers, and, in Lady Wilde's case, as a writer. Wilde's father was an eye/ear surgeon who had an affair with Mary Josephine Travers, who, when he tried to end it, accused him of violating her in his office (claiming she was an ordinary patient). Travers mailed her accusations repeatedly to Lady Wilde, who wrote "a furious letter" to Travers's father. Travers sued Lady Wilde for libel. To give you an idea of how insubstantial the judge found her case, Mary asked for £2,000 and received only one farthing. The case was known throughout the British Isles, and Sir Wilde was ridiculed. He never fully recovered, eventually retreated from life, and died in 1876. We do not know exactly how Wilde reacted throughout his life to his father's infidelities and this court case, but it seems an eerie parallel to Wilde's own eventual demise.

Aside from his position as perhaps the first "modern man" and the scandal surrounding the end of his life, Wilde is remembered as a kind and loving father to his two sons. His youngest, Vyvyan Holland, wrote a book titled *Son of Oscar Wilde* in which he writes,

> Most small boys adore their fathers, and we adored ours; and as all good fathers are, he was a hero to us both . . . There was nothing about him of the monster that some people who never knew him and never even saw him have tried to make him out to be. He was a real companion to us, and we always looked forward eagerly to his frequent visits to our nursery. Most parents in those days were far too solemn and pompous with their children, insisting on a vast amount of usually undeserved respect. My own father was quite different; he had so much of the child in his own nature that he delighted in playing our games. (52)

In this way, too, Wilde lived outside of the Victorian ideals. Of the conviction for gross indecency that led to two years hard labor and the loss of his family and reputation, William Butler Yeats writes, "[Wilde] considered that his crime was not the vice itself, but that he should have brought such misery upon his wife and children, and that he was bound to accept any chance, however slight, to re-establish his position" (173).

However Wilde is remembered as a man, he will always be remembered as a brilliant writer. He is fascinating in part because this one man who wrote in a style sometimes called "bratty didacticism" (Nunokawa 39) is also regarded as the "cleverest person in the world" (2). His work is full of wisdom, and his life a rather triumphant cautionary tale for those considering disobeying society's rules.

HIS INFLUENCES

The first influence on Wilde was surely his mother, Jane Francesca Elgee. She wrote political articles and poems and "embraced the cause of the Irish people in their struggle against English tyranny" (Holland 19). She signed her work "Speranza." It certainly seems fair to say that "If Wilde learned from his father the pleasures of the arresting anecdote and well-turned phrase, his mother taught him the delights of the insurrectionary statement and the dramatic gesture" (Nunokawa 8).

Speranza stood out in a time and place where rebellion (against England, mainly) was common: "She was a fiery champion of nationalism and her writing were wildly inflammatory" (Holland 19). Her response to allegations against Oscar included a letter written in December 1848 in which she wrote: "I should like to rage through life . . . this orthodox creeping is too tame for me, this wild rebellious, ambitious nature of mine" (Nunokawa 8).

Certainly Walter Pater was an enormous influence on Wilde, particularly in terms of the aesthetic philosophies. Pater "preached that physical sensation is an end in itself, to which it is noble to aspire" (Holland 27). Aesthetes "believed that the arts should provide refined sensuous pleasure, rather than convey moral messages, contradicting the popular Victorian belief that art should be something moral or useful" (Nunokawa 5). These versions did not go far enough for Wilde, though, and he spent a lot of time expanding on Pater's work in his own writing. It is important to note that concerning the Aesthetic movement Wilde was both influenced and influential.

Wilde was also greatly affected by France's Théophile Gautier, who coined the phrase "art for art's sake," a saying and concept for which Wilde eventually became sort of a poster child. Wilde's theories did not always follow the "art for art's sake" concepts as clearly as we would like to believe, perhaps because of the myriad other people and theories that influenced his work, including epicureanism, John Keats, Walt Whitman, hedonism, Joris-Karl Huysmans, James McNeill Whistler, Max Beerbohm, Robert Louis Stevenson, Charles Dickens, Samuel Johnson, Edgar Allan Poe, John Ruskin, and his own sons, Cyril and Vyvyan, for whom he wrote stories:

> When he grew tired of playing he would keep us quiet by telling us fairy stories, or tales of adventure, of which he had a never-ending supply. . . . He told us all his own written fairy stories suitably adapted for our young minds, and a great many others as well. . . . And he invented poems in prose for us which, though we may not have always understood their inner meaning, always held us spellbound. (Holland 53, 54)

Whichever influences stand out most prominently in a particular work of Wilde's, it is clear that he is still leaving readers, audiences, and listeners spellbound.

HIS WORK

Wilde's work as a whole clearly shows the influences of his biography and his professional and personal life. A familiarity with his life, however, is not necessary for doing intriguing analysis of Wilde's work. This volume will guide you through general approaches to his fiction. The remainder of this section will discuss some of the notable elements of Wilde's work: the patterns in his use of themes, his construction of character, the history and context of his writing, the philosophy underlying his literature, the many experiments he did with the forms his stories took, and his use of symbolism, imagery, and language.

Themes

There is often an outsider, or a suggestion of those living on the fringes of society, in Wilde's work. Wilde's position as an Irishman in England and a homosexual in the 19th century seems to have solidified his focus on themes regarding the outsider. It also allowed him a certain amount of freedom to criticize those around him. He was a part of the society he critiqued, and yet he was always set apart from them as well.

Other themes in Wilde's work include secrecy, suffering, forgiveness, death, guilt, atonement, justice, danger, love, morality, debt, imagination, religion, transgressive sexuality, self-denial, double lives, sacrifice, matriarchy, lying, and betrayal. There are readers who find Wilde to be completely self-involved and unfeeling, though scholars who make connections between his life and his work, who pay attention to how highly those who knew him spoke of him, and who are able to read between the lines will find that Wilde's work extends far outside of himself. He was looking at society's ills as well as his own imperfections. He was absolving and condemning both himself and the world that surrounded him at the same time.

Themes in Wilde are therefore quite complicated, but all the more fun to investigate thanks to that.

Character

Wilde himself was a "character," in the sense that he was notable as a personality outside of any recognition for his writing. Scholar Russell Jackson writes that Wilde "was a master of what would now be called media opportunities. His epigrammatic, paradoxical utterances made for effective publicity" (164). All of this leaves us wondering which characters of Wilde's contain elements of the man himself.

Of all of his characters, Wilde most famously wrote of three in *The Picture of Dorian Gray*: "Basil Hallward is what I think I am: Lord Henry what the world thinks me: Dorian what I would like to be—in other ages perhaps." Reader and scholars are still puzzling over exactly what Wilde might have meant by that.

It seems that Wilde connected with many of his characters on several levels. He wrote about good versus evil as well as all of the muddy water in between, represented by the guards in *The Ballad of Reading Gaol,* Lady Bracknell in *The Importance of Being Earnest,* and Lord Henry in *The Picture of Dorian Gray.* One might do well to investigate whether this particular brand of Wildean character represents a social class.

Wilde's female characters are often compelling and strong, like Lady Windermere, Salomé, and Cecily. The entire plot centers around women in *The Importance of Being Earnest, An Ideal Husband,* and *Lady Windermere's Fan,* and yet in *The Picture of Dorian Gray* the only notable female character is undeveloped and hardly acknowledged. Wilde's attitudes toward women seem quite changeable from work to work. Perhaps he identified with their fight for equal rights. Perhaps he admired women like his wife, Constance, who wrote and fought for gender equality. Perhaps he resented the position of women, as the accepted and acceptable lovers of men.

History and Context

It is easy to read Wilde without seriously considering the time period in which he lived and wrote. This could be because so many of Wilde's themes, philosophies, and writing styles resonate even today, so many readers feel that knowledge of his history and context is unnecessary. Knowing something about Wilde's personal background as well as the context of his time and the worlds in which his characters lived can add a lot to readings of his work. Wilde's works not only reflect the society in which he lived, they contain quite a lot of criticism as well.

Wilde lived and wrote during the last half of the 19th century, known as the Victorian era. Victorian ideals include earnestness, virtue, morality, restraint—all ideals with which Wilde struggled on some level. As an Irishman, he had a particular relationship with English society as an outsider. As a dandy and eventually a homosexual, Wilde's outsider status was compounded.

Today Wilde is often held up as an example, a hero to the gay community—the first to stand up to society and perform the act that we now call coming out of the closet. What happened in Wilde's time was done and interpreted very differently. Wilde was not just courageously crashing through society's norms; he was dealing with actual laws regarding homosexuality. Though the trials Wilde endured began because of his relationship with Lord Alfred Douglas, Wilde was actually convicted for trysts with rent boys, making his trials and imprisonment a class issue as well. We also know that Wilde's trials and imprisonment led him to write *The Ballad of Reading Gaol,* which is perhaps the most blatant example of societal reform that Wilde ever wrote.

Then consider how Wilde's understanding (or misunderstanding) of himself as a homosexual may have led him to confront issues concerning women's rights and education most directly in *The Importance of Being Earnest.* Did Wilde resent women in some ways, and can that be attributed to his sexual orientation? Did Wilde always identify with outsiders and underdogs?

Studying Wilde can become quite complicated when you consider how his themes, philosophies, biography, style, etc., all tie together. It is difficult, not to say impossible, for example, to completely dissociate Wilde's writing from the world in which he lived and worked. Scholar Robert Merle feels that the connection is undeniable:

> The only character that Wilde created—Dorian Gray—is himself. The only dramatic situation that he described—the sinner threatened by punishment—is his own. The only moral thesis that he seriously upheld—the necessity for forgiveness—is the only one that is of interest to his own case. The only denouement that he foresaw from his anguish—downfall and quasi-voluntary death—is his own destiny. From which arises, in his inspiration, a certain monotony that curiously enough explains and conditions the extreme external variety of his work. (Merle 489–90)

Merle's evaluation circles back on itself, using Wilde's life to describe or explain his art and vice versa. This argument contends that Wilde was writing what he knew in such a way that bled into his eventual philosophies and general ideas about life and art. Presumably, according to this same argument, he could not have come to the same conclusions had he not lived at the end of the Victorian period.

Philosophy and Ideas

Though he could toss off a phrase or observation without appearing to care, Wilde did struggle with philosophical quandaries, and he was not afraid to present such struggles to readers in works like *The Critic as Artist* and *The Decay of Lying*. Even works that can be read purely for entertainment value, like *The Picture of Dorian Gray*, contain much of the philosophical conflict that Wilde recognized in himself and the world around him: "Wilde liked to give the impression that words flowed easily from his pen, but this was part of a strategy for undermining assumptions about the seriousness of art" (Jackson 162). One thing that Wilde always took seriously was art.

Wilde's philosophies included aspects of several important ideas: aestheticism, hedonism, life imitates art, social consciousness, beauty *and* usefulness, power, wealth, and religion. He was perhaps most greatly concerned with the relationship between life and art: "He created a kind of symbiosis of art and life in which it was often difficult to tell which of the elements was the more real and the more significant" (Kohl 1). Wilde's own life, in fact, imitated his art at times, and it seems his art imitated his life in equal part. Even Wilde's son Vyvyan Holland recognized Wilde's preoccupation with philosophies that would eventually help to ruin him: "My father lived in a world of his own; an artificial world, perhaps, but a world in which the only things that really mattered were art and beauty in all their forms. This gave him that horror of conventionality which destroyed him in the end" (54).

Form and Genre

Even though Wilde is known as a flamboyant, funny, entertaining figure and writer, it is important to realize the time and effort he put into his work. Art was a meaningful thing to him—a philosophy of life, in some ways. Whatever genre or form Wilde wrote in, he paid more attention to the words, form, and process than many others have done.

A few of the forms and genres in which Wilde wrote include: myth, poetry, fantasy/fairy tale, novel, essay, letter, farce, social comedy, plays, and social drama. You might say that Wilde was consistently inconsistent—always changing form, genre, and style. And he leaves us with several questions about these aspects of his work. For example, he wrote only one novel, *The Picture of Dorian Gray.* Why not more? He never wrote autobiography—scholars say that *The Ballad of Reading Gaol* came closest. Or was it *The Picture of Dorian Gray*? And what about *De Profundis*? Do we classify that as a private letter or a public declaration?

Wilde's plays were the most successful of all of the forms and genres he tried. Though many were comedies, Wilde took his writing very seriously. Of writing *Lady Windermere's Fan*, he laments, "I am not satisfied with myself or my work. I can't get a grip of the play yet: I can't get my people real. . . . I am very sorry, but artistic work can't be done unless one is in the mood; certainly my work can't. Sometimes I spend months over a thing, and don't do any good; at other times I write a thing in a fortnight" (*Letters* 282).

Wilde scholar Peter Raby makes it clear that "Wilde was a master of conventions, and particularly the conventions of popular form: he did not hesitate to exploit any medium within which he chose to work" ("Wilde's" 144). This exploitation is not necessarily a bad thing. Wilde did help to reinvent or reinvigorate forms and genres that were stale or tired. There probably is not a single work of Wilde's that can be dealt with as one simple category/form/genre. Most of his works need to be pulled even further apart to get at the subcategories or alternate forms. How, for example, does Wilde manage to squeeze both farce and melodrama into his writing for the stage?

Language, Symbols, and Imagery

Reading Wilde's works can seem quite complicated at times because of his use of language, symbols, and imagery. Wilde's genius, in fact, is generally understood to lie in the way that he manipulates language and surpasses readers' expectations. For example, Wilde often uses paradox "as a means of undermining the validity of conventional beliefs" (Kohl 5). The tricky thing about Wilde is remembering that he is not just writing in a particular style to be clever or confusing. He is often writing that way to make a larger point.

Sometimes that larger point that Wilde was trying to make was simply a reinvention of the style in which he was writing. As Norbert Kohl writes, "One need only think of the style of his comedies and his critical essays to realize the degree of originality with which he transmuted whatever material he had inherited" (13). In *The Importance of Being Earnest*, for example, Wilde uses inversion to make his characters look ridiculous and to critique the society in which those characters (and most of his audience members) live. In this same play he is also poking fun at the Victorian social dramas popular at the time. Some scholars claim that much of Wilde's writing contains the language and symbols of homosexuality or homoeroticism. *The Picture of Dorian Gray*, for example, has been read as a homoerotic work in which the language between Basil Hallward and Dorian Gray is particularly charged with sexual tension. You would have to perform a close reading as well as a historical analysis to come to your own conclusions about that. Other scholars claim that such arguments about Wilde's work are anachronistic, and that today's scholars are inappropriately putting their own worldviews onto Wilde's work.

Final Words

Oscar Wilde died on November 30, 1900, and is buried in Paris. His tombstone often appears dirty or smudged in photographs because of the large number of lip prints left on it by visiting admirers. His work is still widely studied and his life still enormously fascinating to audiences of films like *Paris, je t'aime* and plays such as *The Judas Kiss*. For as often and regularly as his life and works have been studied, there is much we will never know about Wilde, who wrote somewhat prophetically: "Every great man nowadays has his disciples, and it is always Judas who writes the biography."

Bibliography

Ellman, Richard. *Oscar Wilde.* New York: Vintage, 1988.

———, ed. *Oscar Wilde: A Collection of Critical Essays.* Twentieth Century Views Series. Englewood Cliffs, NJ: Prentice-Hall, 1969.

Gide, André. *Oscar Wilde.* Trans. Bernard Frechtman. New York: Philosophical Library, 1949.

Holland, Vyvyan. *Son of Oscar Wilde.* London: Rupert Hart-Davis, 1954.

Jackson, Russell. *The Importance of Being Earnest. Cambridge Companion to Oscar Wilde.* Ed. Peter Raby. Cambridge: Cambridge UP, 1997. 161–77.

Kohl, Norbert. *Oscar Wilde: The Works of a Conformist Rebel.* Trans. David Henry Wilson. Cambridge: Cambridge UP, 1989.

Merle, Robert. *Oscar Wilde.* Paris: Library Academique Perrin, 1948.

Newman, Lesléa. Introduction. *Oscar Wilde.* Gay and Lesbian Writers Series. Lesléa Newman, series editor. Philadelphia: Chelsea House, 2005.

Nunokawa, Jeff, and Amy Sickels. *Oscar Wilde.* Gay and Lesbian Writers Series. Lesléa Newman, series editor. Philadelphia: Chelsea House, 2005.

Raby, Peter. *Oscar Wilde.* Cambridge: Cambridge UP, 1988.

———. "Wilde's Comedies of Society." *Cambridge Companion to Oscar Wilde.* Ed. Peter Raby. Cambridge: Cambridge UP, 1997. 143–60.

Wilde, Oscar. *The Letters of Oscar Wilde.* Ed. Rupert Hart-Davis. New York: Harcourt, Brace and World, 1962.

Yeats, W. B. *The Autobiography of William Butler Yeats.* New York: MacMillan, 1953.

THE BALLAD OF READING GAOL

READING TO WRITE

RICHARD ELLMANN, perhaps the most highly respected recent biographer of Oscar Wilde, writes of *The Ballad of Reading Gaol*, "Once read, it is never forgotten" (534). This perception of the poem may come from a wide variety of places: the poem's autobiographical nature, its inspiration from actual events, its status as the only piece Wilde published after his release from prison, not to mention its echoing structure, haunting refrain, and social message. As with any poem, it is possible to read *The Ballad of Reading Gaol* in a stilted, sing-song fashion that may mask its lyricism. But those who have read and studied the poem carefully know of the endless possibilities for study contained within this outwardly simple ballad.

Just the beginning of Part II of the poem gives readers much to work with in terms of reflection and interpretation:

> Six weeks our guardsman walked the yard,
>   In the suit of shabby gray:
> His cricket cap was on his head,
>   And his step seemed light and gay,
> But I never saw a man who looked
>   So wistfully at the day.
>
> I never saw a man who looked
>   With such a wistful eye

Upon that little tent of blue
   Which prisoners call the sky,
   And at every wandering cloud that trailed
   Its raveled fleeces by.

He did not wring his hands, as do
   Those witless men who dare
To try and rear the changeling Hope
   In the cave of black Despair:
He only looked upon the sun,
   And drank the morning air.

He did not wring his hands nor weep,
   Nor did he peek or pine,
But he drank the air as though it held
   Some healthful anodyne;
With open mouth he drank the sun
   As though it had been wine!

And I and all the souls in pain,
   Who tramped the other ring,
Forgot if we ourselves had done
   A great or little thing,
And watched with gaze of dull amaze
   The man who had to swing.

And strange it was to see him pass
   With a step so light and gay,
And strange it was to see him look
   So wistfully at the day,
And strange it was to think that he
   Had such a debt to pay. (97–132)

Certainly the repetition in these lines is one of the first things to stand out. Phrases like "light and gay," "He did not wring his hands," and "And strange it was" are all repeated within this brief excerpt. Others such as "wistfully at the day" are repeated at various points throughout the poem. A paper on repetition in the poem must do more than point out its presence. You will need to determine why particular repetitions or the structure of repetition in general is important. For example, phrases such as "He did not wring his hands" give us a characterization of the man who is to be hanged. What does such a phrase reveal about this man? How does it make readers feel about him? Why? Does Wilde repeat the phrase because he particularly wants readers to feel this way? Why or why not? Writing an effective paper on literature often involves asking questions in order to get started on your research, and then answering those questions in order to have something to support in the paper.

Color is also important in the poem, and this brief section brings in the colors gray, blue, and black. What kind of mood do such colors create? Did they have particular significance for Wilde and/or the prison system? How would readers at the time have responded to Wilde's use of color? Is that response different from that of readers today? Why is the blue sky always connected to wistfulness in the poem? Again, begin your work with questions, and you will find that as you answer them with detailed support from the work, arguments about the poem emerge.

Even the briefest phrase in the poem can lead to intricate levels of interpretation. Wilde calls the prisoners "souls in pain," perhaps because he wants to acknowledge them as people rather than felons or burdens on society. Everyone has a soul, and many people like to believe it is the most important piece of themselves. Referring to prisoners as souls, then, humanizes them to a degree that makes it difficult for readers to deny a connection with or similarity to these prisoners. Why is this connection important to Wilde? What kind of response did it generate from 19th-century readers? What kinds of responses does it generate today? Why?

Finally, the final lines in this section of *The Ballad of Reading Gaol* draw our attention to the reasons this condemned man is imprisoned: "And strange it was to think that he / Had such a debt to pay" (131–32). We cannot help but wonder if Wilde is purposely begging questions here. The use of the word "debt" to describe imprisonment is a common one. Prisoners are paying a "debt to society" as we see it. Perhaps the word stands out here juxtaposed with the man's "light and gay" step and his wistful gazing. Perhaps Wilde wants readers to acknowledge themselves as the society to which this man's debt will be paid. In that light, it seems almost silly to think that because this man killed his wife he now owes something to you and to me. We begin to ask questions that Wilde would likely be happy to hear: Why is society so involved in matters of legality and justice? Are court systems truly fair, or can people be condemned on the basis of public opinion? To what extent is the legal and prison system used to make people on the outside feel superior to those condemned within?

There is much more to be done with this section of the poem and the poem as a whole. This is Wilde's most blatant work of social literature or art intended to influence laws or society and have an impact extending beyond its own beauty. This seems to contradict Wilde's aesthetic "art for art's sake" mantra, until we remember that Wilde was rarely straightforward about or within his work, making the complexities within numerous and exciting. Seamus Heaney says that "the ballad represents a withdrawal from the pursuit of pure style in order that impure content might be given a better showing . . . [this poem shows] the moment of crisis when an aesthete, under pressure of intense pain, mutates into a propagandist" (40). This propaganda was wildly popular. Published anonymously (under the name C.3.3., indicating Wilde's prison number) on February 13, 1898, the poem was reprinted the same month. Seven editions had been published by June 1899, when Wilde's name first appeared on the poem (Horodisch 14).

This poem is the only instance in Wilde's writing where his life is such a blatant inspiration. Certainly critics have made many biographical inferences into Wilde's other works, but *Ballad* is the only work that Wilde openly stated came from his life experiences. As one scholar writes, "Wilde did not treat a literary theme but gave poetic expression to a real experience" (13).

TOPICS AND STRATEGIES

This section of the chapter addresses various possible topics for writing about *The Ballad of Reading Gaol* as well as general methods for approaching these topics. These lists are in no way exhaustive and are meant to provide a jumping-off point rather than an answer key. Use these suggestions to find your own ideas and form your own analyses. All topics discussed in this chapter could turn into very effective papers.

Themes

A theme in a literary work is an idea, an action, an occurrence, or a system that in some way threads itself throughout the book. Themes are often identifiable through a close reading of words, phrases, ideas, and even chapter titles, and they are recognizable as something about which the character(s) and/or author appear to have much to say. In other words, if a book's action and/or characters continually return to a similar idea, you have probably identified a theme of the book.

Wilde biographer Richard Ellmann writes, "The poem has a divided theme: the cruelty of the doomed murderer's crime, the insistence that such cruelty is pervasive; and the greater cruelty of his punishment by a guilty society" (532). Do you agree? Why or why not?

Sample Topics:

1. **Man's inhumanity to man:** How does each "character" in the poem somehow harm others?

   Seamus Heaney writes that "the poem not only condemns the penal system but also insinuates that each reader is guilty within the cell of his or her secret being" (48). We find such ideas in lines like, "That every prison that men build / Is built with bricks of shame, / And bound with bars Lest Christ should see / How men their brothers maim" (549–52). Not only do these lines refer to the convicts (sometimes murderers) within the prison walls, they also refer to those who maim their brothers by building the walls (literal and figurative) in the first place. What kinds of "walls" exist between prisoners and guards, prisoners and other prisoners, prisoners and the outside world? Which incidents seem intentional, and which ones can't be helped? What message does Wilde want readers to walk away with concerning such inhumanity? How can we tell?

2. **Guilt:** Does Wilde leave anyone out? Are there any innocent parties in the poem and its readership?

   It seems that everyone in the poem is equally guilty for a variety of reasons: "Yet each man kills the thing he loves, / By each let this be heard" (37–38). What effect do lines like these have on readers? If readers are supposed to feel guilty after reading the poem, why was/is it so popular? Is this Wilde's way of expressing his own guilt, or is his point that he is no guiltier than anyone else in or out of prison?

3. **Justice:** How does Wilde's portrayal of the prison reveal both justice and injustice, within the prison itself and/or society in general?

Wilde biographer Richard Ellmann writes of *The Ballad of Reading Gaol* that "As in his plays, sin was shown to be evenly distributed round the globe, though justice was not" (532). Wilde pointedly uses the word "each" to make his point all-inclusive: "For each man kills the thing he loves, / yet each man does not die" (53–54). Who in the poem is punished, and who commits crime yet gets away with it?

Character

When studying characters, there are several angles to take. You might look at character development or what distinguishes one character from another. How does Wilde differentiate between any two characters? You might also investigate change in a character, noting when a character seems to evolve (or devolve) in some way. How, for instance, does the narrator change over the course of the poem? Does his general personality change or does the world around him change? Or both? Along the same lines, you can choose to study a character who perhaps should change but does not.

It is always fascinating to study the ways in which a character is created. This requires you to look at specific words, phrases, settings, or moods that surround and help describe a character in order to see how Wilde helps readers form appropriate opinions of his characters.

Character is a very interesting aspect of *The Ballad of Reading Gaol,* partly because many characters in the poem do not have names. So readers are forced to ask if these characters are meant as representatives of an entire group of people (namely guards and prisoners), or whether they all somehow represent Wilde in his conflicting roles both in and out of prison. Or perhaps Wilde simply wanted to keep his inspirations for the characters anonymous and therefore made identifying them nearly impossible. Who are the characters? Is one of them Wilde? Is more than one of them Wilde? Which ones should/will readers identify with? Why?

Sample Topics:

1. **Prisoners:** In what ways is the narrator both similar to and different from the other prisoners?

   Is Wilde's characterization of prisoners too empathetic (sympathetic)? The soldier who is hanged in the poem did kill his wife, and yet the poem evokes sympathy and compassion for him. Why? How does Wilde (whether or not he is the narrator) characterize himself in the poem? Why?

2. **Guards:** In what ways does Wilde avoid casting the guards as the bad guys? Are readers expected/asked to feel sorry for them too? Why or why not?

   What kinds of associations does Wilde create with the guards, particularly concerning possibly symbolic colors? How do the guards treat the prisoners? In what ways does Wilde portray the guards as prisoners too? One of the warders (prison guards) who encountered Wilde at Reading Gaol wrote about Wilde's imprisonment. Reading this piece might provide compelling insight into Wilde's reasons for characterizing guards the way he does in *The Ballad of Reading Gaol*. (The piece is available in Robert Harborough Sherard's *The Life of Oscar Wilde*.)

3. **Narrator:** Is it Wilde? Why is Wilde's relationship with the narrator so important?

   Seamus Heaney writes, "The poem can bestow no final liberation upon either the speaker or the condemned man . . . because the speaker is the condemned man" (45). If the speaker (narrator) is the condemned man, then where does Wilde fit in? Certainly Wilde had reason to feel condemned as well, making it easy to see how we can conflate the narrator, the condemned man, and Wilde. Do you think Wilde intentionally makes it difficult to separate the characters from one another? Why or why not? Do you think Wilde wants us to associate his actual prison experiences and feelings with characters in the poem? Why or why not? Consider that the poem was originally published anonymously.

History and Context

Perhaps the broadest category of writing about literature, studying history and context compels you to research the actual circumstances surrounding the action in the poem and/or the process of writing the poem.

The Ballad of Reading Gaol is difficult to categorize alongside Wilde's other work, since it is the only piece published after his imprisonment. It is different for other reasons as well: "It is a new style for me, full of actuality and life in its directness of message and meaning" (Wilde *Letters* 630). The importance of the poem's social commentary is enhanced by knowledge of its history and context, in terms of Wilde's own experiences and the 19th-century society and prison system in general.

An additional tie to Wilde's life lies in the fact that part of the poem is now inscribed on Wilde's tombstone:

> And alien tears will fill for him
> For his mourners will be outcast men,
> And outcasts always mourn.

Was Wilde an outcast man as well? In what ways? How does this affect his writing of *The Ballad of Reading Gaol*? How does it affect our reading of the poem?

Sample Topics:

1. **British penal system:** What are the major flaws in the penal system according to Wilde's poem?

The system in *The Ballad of Reading Gaol* punishes everyone. All had good intentions, but it is not working because "It is only what is good in Man / That wastes and withers there" (561–62). There is no chance for reform in the prison Wilde portrays, only silence (from each other, guards, society, God?). Readers cannot help but feel something for the prisoners when they come across the lines, "Something was dead in each of us, / And what was dead was Hope" (359–60). This is a system that imprisons people in debt, taking away whatever earning potential they may have had and necessitating work by wives and children who remain outside of prison but are now solely responsible for paying off the debts. Wilde was imprisoned for what was basically a lifestyle choice—what many today would argue should not be anyone's business outside of Wilde's own intimate circle. Who seems to be at fault here, in terms of the failure of the penal system? Why? How does Wilde keep from indicting the guards?

2. **Charles Thomas Wooldridge:** Why does Wilde choose this story to tell, rather than focusing on his own?

Wooldridge was a Royal Horse Guardsman (a regiment of the British army) who was tried and convicted of murdering his wife and executed at Reading on July 7, 1896. Wilde did not witness the execution, though it is clearly the inspiration for the poem, given his epigraph: In Memoriam C.T.W. The actual murder took place on a road and not in a bed, as Wilde writes, so we know that he took some creative license. Why is Wilde so fascinated by this particular prisoner? Is he more horrified or more empathetic? To what extent does Wilde (the narrator?) seem able to relate to Wooldridge?

3. **Prison conditions:** Why does Wilde choose this subject to write his most blatant social indictment?

Wilde's letter to the *Daily Chronicle* of May 27, 1897 reads, "With bars they blur the gracious moon, / And blind the goodly sun: / And they do well to hide their Hell, / For in it things are done / That son of God nor son of Man / Ever should look upon!" (553–58). These things had been a concern for Charles Dickens too. The treadmill, which Wilde worked on, was a bit like today's StairMaster. Prisoners got on the machine and "climbed" in order to generate power for mills. There were walls between treadmills so that prisoners had to work in isolation, the idea being that they would spend their (usually six-hour) shifts on the treadmill searching their souls and learning to repent their crimes. Wilde writes of it in *The Ballad*: "We banged the tins, and bawled the hymns, / And sweated on the mill" (225–26). Prisoners (including Wilde) also often picked oakum, which is basically pulling apart old ropes in order to pull out the loose fibers. Wilde was transferred to a few different prisons, so that by the time he got to the last—Reading—he was not well enough for manual labor. But he had not forgotten his previous experiences. *Pit of Shame: The Real Ballad of Reading Gaol* by Anthony Stokes provides rich historical information about Reading Gaol in particular and prison conditions in general.

Philosophy and Ideas

Philosophy and ideas in a novel are similar to theme, but they are more general, or more universal. Writing about the philosophy and ideas in a book means that you identify broad philosophical ideas and investigate the ways in which the book comments on them. *The Ballad of Reading Gaol* seems to negate Wilde's earlier philosophies. Wilde was "uncomfortable about drawing the poem 'from personal experience, a sort of denial of my own philosophy of art in many ways'" (Ellmann 534). This poem is not art for art's sake. Or is it? It is in line with *The Importance of Being Earnest* and other pieces clearly intended to open readers' eyes to their own worlds, holding up a mirror to themselves and their society.

Sample Topics:

1. **Theology:** In what way is Wilde commenting on theology in *The Ballad of Reading Gaol*?

   Many scholars have read the hanged man in *The Ballad* as a Christ figure. It is an interpretation made all the more interesting by the fact that after his release from prison, Wilde began to develop ties with religion, specifically Catholicism. God and other religious imagery are mentioned a number of times in the poem. Wilde portrays cruel treatment by humans in society and in prison, but "a broken and contrite heart / The Lord will not despise" (623–24). Does Wilde (and the narrator, if you feel they are different voices) seem to be a believer in Christianity, or is there some cynicism in the poem? What does Wilde/narrator seem to want readers to think and feel about theology? How can we tell?

Form and Genre

The way in which a book is written and presented can have an enormous impact on readers' reception and interpretations. The form that a work takes involves its shape and structure—chapter length, format, etc. A work's genre is its classification.

Seamus Heaney writes that in *The Ballad of Reading Gaol*, "fact and fiction combine in a way that the younger Wilde would have thoroughly disapproved of" (42). In what ways do fact and fiction work together to make this poem more powerful than it would be if it were only one or the other?

Wilde himself writes about the poem, claiming that it "suffers under the difficulty of a divided aim in style. Some is realistic, some is romantic: some poetry, some propaganda. I feel it keenly, but as a whole I think the production interesting: that it is interesting from more points of view than one is artistically to be regretted" (Wilde *Letters* 654).

Sample Topics:

1. **Ballad:** Is the ballad the most effective form for Wilde's message? Why or why not?

   A ballad traditionally contains "naïveté of expression, a certain laxity in the rhymes" (Sherard 413). *The Ballad of Reading Gaol* is a historical ballad with high audience appeal because it is memorable and rhythmic. Seamus Heaney writes that Wilde's poem hearkens back to earlier times: "there is something entirely conventional about his subject of murder and retribution, the setting of gaol yard and gaol cell, the case of warder and hangman and chaplain, the dreadful people of gallows and quicklimed grave—all of which things belong in the tradition of the broadside ballad" (45).

2. **Fiction/nonfiction:** What does the blend of fiction and nonfiction add to or take away from the poem?

Wilde is rarely completely straightforward, so read this excerpt from one of his letters with an ear for cynicism: "I, of course, feel that the poem is too autobiographical and that *real* experiences are alien things that should never influence one, but it was wrung out of me, a cry of pain" (*Letters* 708). Does Wilde really believe that fiction and autobiography must always be completely separate? How does *The Ballad of Reading Gaol* help to answer this question by serving as an example? Why didn't Wilde just write a straightforward account of only his own experiences?

3. **Propaganda:** What does Wilde seem to want readers to take away from their readings of the poem?

Wilde's letter to Robert Ross: "You are quite right in saying that the poem should end at 'outcasts always mourn,' but the propaganda, which I desire to make, begins there" (*Letters* 661). Propaganda is "a set of messages aimed at influencing the opinions or behaviors of a large number of people." Wilde was out of prison by the time he wrote *The Ballad of Reading Gaol*, yet clearly he has much to express about his experiences. What action might he want readers to take after reading *The Ballad of Reading Gaol*? How well does Wilde make his arguments? Is the propaganda really contained in these final sections of the poem, or is it pervasive?

Language, Symbols, and Imagery

To effectively study language, symbols, and imagery you must move beyond unnecessary summary to investigate how the poem is written and then make speculations about how these methods of writing and literary elements affect the content of the poem.

Far removed as we are from late 19th-century prison life, Wilde brings that world to life for us in *The Ballad of Reading Gaol*. His choices in language, symbols, and imagery allow readers to more concretely envision the life of Reading Gaol.

Sample Topics:

1. Colors: What significance do individual colors have in the poem?

The first color mentioned in the poem is scarlet/red, tying together the soldier's coat, wine, and blood. Soon after, Wilde mentions the colors gray, blue, and silver. Do certain types of people or certain moods get equated with particular colors? Why? How does Wilde's use of color help to develop the imagery in the poem? Consider that Wilde was known as a dandy and often wore unusual colors. He was and still is described with the term "colorful." How might the colors in Wilde's life have influenced his use of color in the poem?

2. Guardsmen: Why is it important for readers to find some humanity in the guards—to feel some measure of sympathy or empathy for them?

In *Ballad* Wilde writes, "For he to whom a watcher's doom / Is given as his task, / Must set a lock upon his lips, / And make his face a mask" (201–04). In what ways do the guardsmen symbolize all of humanity? The narrator (whether or not you believe it is Wilde himself) and the guards are all watching the condemned man for various reasons. How do lines such as these draw similarities between the narrator and the guards?

3. Repetition: How does repetition help readers identify themes in the work?

Just a few instances of repetition in the poem include: "I never saw a man who looked" (11), "Each man kills the thing he loves" (53), and "all men kill the thing they love" (649). Why are some words, lines, or ideas important enough to repeat? This is a ballad, after all. To what extent does Wilde use repetition to form a sort of chorus, or refrain, that ties the story together?

4. **Opposites:** Why is it perhaps more effective for Wilde to mention and deal with opposite images rather than simply focusing on one or the other?

Wilde juxtaposes several images and ideas in the poem, including "night and day . . . community and isolation" (McLeer 42). How does the expression of community help readers better understand prisoners' isolation? What does reading about daytime tell us about the nights?

Compare and Contrast Essays

We can often get a clearer idea of what something is by understanding what it is not, and vice versa. Papers that use comparison and contrast methods include not just lists of similarities and differences but theories and interpretations about why such similarities and differences exist, and what effect they have on the poem as a whole.

Sample Topics:

1. **Wilde's prison experience and the experiences in the poem:** What is historically accurate and what is not? Does it really matter if it is true?

   What does knowledge of Wilde's autobiography add to (or take away from) a reading of *The Ballad of Reading Gaol*? Does Wilde seem to be equating his crimes (and punishment) with those of a murderer? Is this useful, or does it seem as though Wilde is overdramatizing his own experience?

2. **Guards and prisoners:** Is the relationship between guards and prisoners the most important aspect of *Ballad*? Why or why not?

   Perhaps a key question here is whether Wilde seems to be drawing more parallels than differences between guards and prisoners. Answer that question and then ask why Wilde would do such a thing. Is he trying to universalize these experiences?

Is he lamenting his own days in prison and writing a laundry list of grievances?

3. Wilde's version and W. B. Yeats's version: What effect does each version have on readers? Why?

In his 1936 edition of *The Oxford Book of Modern Verse,* Yeats keeps 38 of Wilde's original 109 stanzas. What themes, ideas, and messages are present in Wilde's version and absent in Yeats's (or vice versa)? Look up the history of Yeats's revisions to learn his reasons for the changes.

Bibliography for *The Ballad of Reading Gaol*

Ellmann, Richard. *Oscar Wilde.* New York: Vintage Books, 1988.

Heaney, Seamus. "Speranza in Reading: On the Ballad of Reading Gaol." *The Island Magazine* 62 (1995): 40–48.

Horodisch, Abraham. *Oscar Wilde's Ballad of Reading Gaol: A Bibliographical Study.* New York: Aldus Book Co., 1954.

McLeer, Karen. "Keep It Wild(e): Reclaiming Reader Expectation in 'Reading Gaol'." *The European Studies Journal* 14.1 (1997): 37–46.

Raby, Peter. *Oscar Wilde.* Cambridge: Cambridge UP, 1988.

Shaw, George Bernard. "My Memories of Oscar Wilde." *Oscar Wilde.* By Frank Harris. New York: Carroll & Graf, 1992. 329–43.

Sherard, Robert Harborough. *The Life of Oscar Wilde.* London: T. Werner Laurie, 1906.

Stokes, Anthony. *The Pit of Shame: The Real Ballad of Reading Gaol.* Winchester: Waterside Press, 2007.

Wilde, Oscar. *The Ballad of Reading Gaol.* 1898. *Oscar Wilde: The Major Works.* Ed. Isobel Murray. Oxford: Oxford UP, 1989. 518–66.

THE CRITIC AS ARTIST

READING TO WRITE

THE FIRST question to ask about *The Critic as Artist* concerns one of the first things readers notice about the work: Why does Wilde divide it into two parts? It is important, in this case, to make careful note of the subtitles for each part (Part One: *With Some Remarks upon the importance of doing nothing;* Part Two: *With some remarks upon the importance of discussing everything*).

At the heart of *The Critic as Artist* lies some of Wilde's philosophies concerning art, life, and criticism. He does not seem to be in a hurry to answer questions but rather wants to highlight the dilemmas themselves, as scholars have noted: "Wilde's esthetics have been, among younger thinkers, the starting-point of a constant discussion of art and literature" (Roditi 225). What kinds of discussion does the following passage inspire?

Ernest. Your theory of education is delightful. But what influence will your critic, brought up in these exquisite surroundings, possess? Do you really think that any artist is ever affected by criticism?

Gilbert. The influence of the critic will be the mere fact of his own existence. He will represent the flawless type. In him the culture of the century will see itself realized. You must not ask of him to have any aim other than the perfecting of himself. The demand of the intellect, as has been well said, is simply to feel itself alive. The critic may, indeed, desire to exercise influence; but, if so, he will concern himself not with the individual, but with the age, which he will seek to wake into consciousness, and to make responsive, creating in it new desires and appetites, and lending it his larger vision and his nobler moods. The actual art of today will occupy him less than the art of tomorrow, far less than the art of yesterday, and as for this or that person at present toiling away, what do the industrious matter? They do their best, no doubt, and consequently we get the worst from them. It is always with the best intentions that the worst work is done. And besides, my dear Ernest, when a man reaches the age of forty, or becomes a Royal Academician, or is elected a member of the Athenaeum Club or is recognized as a popular novelist, whose books are in great demand at suburban railway stations, one may have the amusement of exposing him, but one cannot have the pleasure of reforming him. And this is, I dare say, very fortunate for him; for I have no doubt that reformation is a much more painful process than punishment, is indeed punishment in its most aggravated and moral form—a fact which accounts for our entire failure as a community to reclaim that interesting phenomenon who is called the confirmed criminal. (290)

There are overtones in this passage of the Industrial Revolution, indicating that a historical perspective might be in order when writing your paper. Think about Gilbert's question, "what do the industrious matter?" Is Wilde indicating simply the hardworking artist here, or does he intentionally use language of the Industrial Revolution to call to mind factory workers and others who may be industrious indeed but largely ignored by upper classes and, in some cases, government. The larger question then becomes, to what extent, if at all, is *The Critic as Artist* a social or political critique of late 19th-century England?

How much of what Wilde writes in this passage (and indeed in the entire work) is personal for him? He certainly endured criticism for his life and his work. Are his feelings about that reflected in Gilbert's words here? How can we tell?

An anonymous reviewer in Wilde's time wrote that "[Wilde] has written a fascinating, stimulating book, with more common sense in it than he would perhaps care to be accused of" ("Unsigned" 92). What would Wilde's first readers have understood to be "common sense"? Are lines like "It is always with the best intentions that the worst work is done" common sense? Is this what Wilde intended?

Another question to consider is how readers of Wilde's time read and understood this piece. We know that many readers and critics at the time understood Wilde's importance and potential influence: "Mr. Wilde can hardly hope to become popular by proposing real study to people burning to impart their ignorance; but the criticism that develops in the mind a more subtle quality of apprehension and discernment is the criticism that creates the intellectual atmosphere of the age" (Repplier 106). What was the general response to *The Critic as Artist*? Why? Did this response impact Wilde's subsequent work?

TOPICS AND STRATEGIES

This section of the chapter addresses various possible topics for writing about *The Critic as Artist* as well as general methods for approaching these topics. These lists are in no way exhaustive and are meant to provide a jumping-off point rather than an answer key. Use these suggestions to find your own ideas and form your own analyses. All topics discussed in this chapter could turn into very effective papers.

Themes

A theme is not just something that the written work mentions or even dwells upon—it is something (an idea, etc.) about which the writer has something in particular to say. You can find a theme by looking for an idea or subject that threads its way through much of a work or is repeated in some fashion throughout the work. Which topics/ideas do Gilbert and Ernest seem to dwell on? Where do you suspect you hear Wilde's voice and opinion coming through? Why? What does he say? You can also look at the question of why a particular theme is so strong in the story. This line of questioning involves additional research into Wilde's time period and possibly his intentions for writing.

Sample Topics:

1. **Aesthetic criticism:** In what ways does aesthetic criticism become a theme in *The Critic as Artist* rather than a theory that Wilde himself is using? Or is aestheticism both a theme and an espoused theory, in this case?

Wilde scholars and critics have much to say about the theme of aesthetic criticism: "Wilde condemned the unintelligent and the unbeautiful just as a moralist condemns the sinful, because the unintelligent, the unbeautiful and the sinful or evil had become one and the same" (Roditi 217). Lawrence Danson claims that "Wilde's new version of the old aestheticism deploys subjectivity, individuality and the autonomy of art against the supposed objectivity and professionalism of 19th-century science and its offshoot in literature, realism" (85).

2. **Masks:** What does Wilde say about masks in *The Critic as Artist*?

Wilde mentions masks directly and indirectly a number of times in *The Critic as Artist*: "Man is least himself when he talks in his own person. Give him a mask and he will tell you the truth" (282); "What people call insincerity is simply a method by which we can multiply our personalities" (285). Wilde uses the concept of masks in much of his writing—to such an extent that scholars wonder how much Wilde considered his own life and conduct a series of masks, to some degree. Yet we all probably recognize the wisdom—recognize ourselves—in these discussions of masks. The theme of masks is prevalent in *The Critic as Artist*, bringing up questions regarding the nature of insincerity. How do we know when people (including ourselves) are being sincere? Does it even matter whether or not people are sincere? Is it only the impression of sincerity that we need?

Character

The dialogue form requires that characters become highlighted at the same time as it forces characters to stand behind the words—the dialogue—themselves. Wilde gives very little setting, and there is no plot per se. So what do we learn about the characters? Can we trust what they tell us, since we have no other voices or action against which to weigh their words? Does one character seem more likeable than another? More knowledgeable? How can we tell? What about Wilde's writing leads us to such conclusions?

One method for studying character is to look at the writer's word choices, syntax, etc., and think about how those choices help to frame or round out a character. How does Wilde differentiate between Gilbert and Ernest? Do either of the characters seem to express Wilde's own thoughts and feelings? How can you tell?

Sample Topics:

1. **Gilbert:** He does most of the talking. Does that make it safe to assume that he is the one Wilde wants us to listen to?

   How can we tell when Gilbert is being sincere and when he is just having fun? Ernest says to him, "I wonder do you really believe what you say" (289). Does Gilbert come to represent a particular person or even a group of people? How can you tell? Are we supposed to like Gilbert? Why or why not? Does it matter whether we like him or not?

2. **Ernest:** Does Ernest genuinely accept Gilbert's ideas, or is he perhaps humoring Gilbert or being taken in by the intensity of the conversation?

   When Ernest says, "While you talk it seems to me to be so," it makes it sound like Ernest may not agree with Gilbert once he is given more time to consider (259). Is Ernest actually the voice of reason? Is Ernest the true critic? Is Ernest actually Wilde's conscience?

3. **Wilde:** Can Wilde himself be considered a character?

   Is he somehow a narrator, even though the piece is written as a dialogue? Where can you find Wilde's voice/opinion coming through? Does Wilde stand as a character on his own, or does he embody Gilbert or Ernest? If so, which one? Why? It seems that Wilde had a hard time removing himself completely from any of his writing. Yet we might also wonder if this has more to do with our methods of reading than his methods of writing. Is Wilde really so present in *The Critic as Artist,* or do we simply want and/or need him to be there, perhaps so we can try to figure him out?

History and Context

In this piece Wilde is both directly commenting on his own era and influenced by previous writers, thinkers, and eras. History can help us understand what is influencing Wilde here, and context can help us learn about his more immediate surroundings as well as his influence in his own time. What would *The Critic as Artist* look like and cover if it were written today? Why?

Wilde adds an interesting angle to the issues of history and context, because he was changing and creating a particular historical context even as he was living through it. So then we ask both how history and context influence Wilde and his works as well as how Wilde and his works influence history and context.

Sample Topics:

1. **The Industrial Revolution:** Does Wilde seem to have a particular message about the Industrial Revolution, or does it simply leak into his language because it is such a part of his consciousness?

   The Industrial Revolution of Victorian England is certainly reflected in Wilde's language: "Each little thing we do passes into the great machine of life which may grind our virtues to powder and make them worthless" (257); "We live in the age of the overworked, and the undereducated; the age in which people are so industrious that they become absolutely stupid" (298). Wilde's writing shows the transition being made between Victorian England at the height of the Industrial Revolution and the new, modern century to come.

2. **Chinese philosopher Chuang Tzu:** How is Tzu's philosophy highlighted in *The Critic as Artist*?

   Wilde reviewed Tzu's work in an essay titled, "The Soul of Man Under Socialism," and he mentions him explicitly in *The Critic as Artist.* Taoism emphasizes moderation, humility, and compassion, which we can plainly see would collide with hedonism, another philosophy Wilde often addresses and adopts. Tzu lived around the fourth century B.C. and believed that things are relative. Death, for example, is not necessarily a bad thing. Edouard Roditi claims that "the discovery of Taoism made it possible for Wilde to transcend at last the political dilemmas of the dandy in a new creed of his own" (150). Wilde writes, "The contemplative life, the life that has for its aim not *doing* but *being* and not *being* merely, but *becoming*—that is what the critical spirit can give us" (277). Does Wilde (or Gilbert or Ernest) seem to believe that such a state can be achieved? Are certain types or classes of people more likely than others to achieve it? In what ways does this philosophy surface in Wilde's other works? What if a person is only motivated by their own desire, like Lord Henry in *The Picture of Dorian Gray*?

3. **Wilde's influences:** In what ways would the reception and popularity of these other writers affect Wilde's own reception and popularity?

"Wilde's style has been called 'anthological,' and 'The Critic as Artist,' which welcomes so many voices into the dialogue . . . shows why the adjective is apt" (Danson 88). Wilde directly or indirectly refers to work of Matthew Arnold, Walter Pater, Ralph Waldo Emerson, James Whistler, and Robert Browning, among others. How does his use of these other writers help to inform us of the history and context of *The Critic as Artist*? Why does Wilde refer primarily to other men rather than women?

Philosophy and Ideas

Writing about the philosophy and ideas found in a text is similar to writing about the text's theme, except that philosophy and ideas are applied more generally and live in some sense outside of the text, as well. So when writing about a work's philosophy and ideas, you are looking for the ways in which the work comments on general ideas.

Philosophy and ideas are particularly apt in this work, as one scholar writes, "There is no plot or action, in these dialogues, save those of philosophical discussion" (Roditi 92). Wilde can create and wrestle with various philosophies in ways that boggle a lesser mind. He sometimes manages to simplify and complicate philosophies all at once. And some of the philosophies, such as "Art for art's sake," with which Wilde is most closely associated, become increasingly problematic as we perform close readings on Wilde's works.

Sample Topics:

1. **Individualism:** Is Wilde promoting individualism in *The Critic as Artist*?

   Wilde writes of individualism in a number of ways: "When a great actor plays Shakespeare . . . His own individuality becomes a vital part of the interpretation" (269); "It is through the voice of one crying in the wilderness that the ways of the gods must be prepared" (279). Edouard Roditi writes, "When absolute individualism is thus identified with absolute universality or impassivity as an individual, self-expression is almost identical with . . . loss of self; and an esthetics founded on these principles must inevitably lead . . . to the transcendental inaction of contemplation which *The Critic as Artist* advocates" (218). Lawrence Danson adds that "Wilde's critic as artist fights a battle on behalf of the uncredentialised, unenforceable, self-crediting individual" (85).

2. **Contemplative life:** How does Wilde propose that criticism can help us achieve the contemplative life? How does he make this particular connection?

   Wilde writes that "the life that has for its aim not *doing* but *being*, and not merely, but *becoming*—that is what the critical spirit can give us" (277). Like most of us, Wilde seemed to strive for the contemplative life rather than actually live it. As leisurely as his life may seem to us now, the pace at which he wrote indicates that Wilde and his mind were always working.

3. **Art's unity:** What is it about Art that requires unification, according to Wilde and/or his characters in *The Critic as Artist*?

Consider the following statement very carefully: "It is through Art, and through Art only, that we can realize our perfection; through Art, and through Art only, that we can shield ourselves from the sordid perils of actual existence" (274). What exactly does this mean? How can you tell?

Form and Genre

Form and genre provide ways of classifying works that usually allow us to study them more fully. Form is defined as the style and structure of a work, whereas genre is the type, or classification, of a work. Both form and genre are usually distinct from a work's content, though writers use each of them quite specifically in order to convey a particular message, reach a certain audience, or to simply strengthen the impact of their work. Gilbert comments on this in *The Critic as Artist*: "Form is everything. It is the secret of life. Find expression for a sorrow, and it will become dear to you. Find expression for a joy, and you intensify its ecstasy" (289). Are these Wilde's sentiments too? How can you tell?

Critics and scholars debate about why Wilde chose to write *The Critic as Artist* in dialogue form rather than a novel, play, or even a poem: "A more experienced dialectician and craftsman in this dramatic art of exposition would have presented his material with a greater number of participants; and this would have enhanced the mythopoeic quality of the fictional form and strengthened its devices by varying the points of view . . . so that the argument's verisimilitude would have been greater in the eyes of readers whose points of view vary and whose objections may not all be voiced by Wilde's one character and disposed of by the other" (Roditi 89).

Sample Topics:

1. **Dialogue:** Why would Wilde choose to write a dialogue rather than an essay, which may be viewed as more straightforward?

Do you agree that "the argument is perhaps too long and complex to be successfully expounded and discussed in a dialogue which has but two participants" (88)? Is Wilde hiding behind the characters in the dialogue, or do the two points of view help Wilde to demonstrate the nuance and complications of the issues? Wilde writes that through the dialogue form, the thinker "can both reveal and conceal himself, and give form to every fancy, and reality to every mood. By its means he can exhibit the object from each point of view, and show it to us in the round, as a sculptor shows us things, gaining in this manner all the richness and reality of effect that comes from those side issues that are suddenly suggested by the central idea in its progress, and really illuminate the idea more completely, or from those felicitous after-thoughts that give a fuller completeness to the central scheme, and yet convey something of the delicate charm of chance" (283).

2. **Aphorisms:** Do aphorisms makes the dialogue more realistic, or less? Why?

Wilde uses a number of aphorisms, including: "Oh! journalism is unreadable, and literature is not read" (248); "When people agree with me I always feel that I must be wrong" (292). There are sections (such as page 248) where it seems that Gilbert speaks only in aphorisms. What effect does this have on the argument? On our characterization of Gilbert? Aphorisms, or epigrams, were a specialty of Wilde's, in both his speech and his writing. So this manner of speaking for Gilbert brings him closer, in many scholars' minds, to being the mouthpiece of Wilde. And yet, knowing Wilde, he would have realized that readers would make such a connection and written Gilbert's dialogue this way anyway, simply to throw readers off track and make it more difficult to distinguish Wilde's true opinions.

3. **Paradox:** What affect does Wilde's use of paradox have on readers?

Wilde writes several paradoxes in *The Critic as Artist*: "It is because Humanity has never known where it was going that it has been able to find its way" (257); "nothing that one can imagine is worth doing, and . . . one can imagine everything" (274). Edouard Roditi notes that it is "to Wilde's satirical wit and paradox we owe a whole tradition of literature, though its basic seriousness has not yet been fully appreciated" (226). What kinds of traditions in writing have come out of Wilde's use of paradox? At first the paradoxes seem like nonsense, but closer reading reveals more: "Any fool can talk plain sense and understand it, but it needs a quite superior order of intelligence to disguise sense as nonsense and to see through the disguise" ("Unsigned" 91).

Language, Symbols, and Imagery

Literary works (especially those by someone as talented as Wilde) deserve to be studied not only for their content but for their style as well. This requires you to avoid summarizing the text unnecessarily and focus instead on the ways in which the work is written. It no longer concerns what the work is about but rather how it is written. Studying the language of a text allows you to look carefully at things like syntax, word choice, and general diction. You might, for example, study the various accents and colloquialisms expressed by characters in *The Critic as Artist* to help you delve more deeply into Wilde's characterizations. What does a character's use of language reveal about him/her? Language might also mean a search into the words most commonly used to describe a character, a setting, or an activity. Look at the tone (or mood) surrounding Gilbert and Ernest, for example, and pinpoint elements of language that help to create that tone. Then take it a step further by discussing why it is significant that such a mood is connected with these particular characters.

Imagery includes the details in a story that can be perceived by one or more of the five senses. Wilde's use of imagery is particularly fascinating because he not only uses the technique, he mentions the use of it in his writing as well. An anonymous reviewer writes, "it is in the simplicity of [Wilde's] technique that his art is truly great" ("Unsigned" 91). Do you agree?

Sample Topics:

1. **Questions:** How do these questions help characterize Gilbert and Ernest? How do they allow Wilde to organize the dialogue?

The dialogue form helps Wilde use questions to guide readers and make his points. Ernest asks Gilbert, "What is the use of art-criticism?" (243). Later Ernest asks, "What are the two supreme and highest arts?" (249). Gilbert, on the other hand, asks mainly rhetorical questions or questions for which he already has an answer: "What is our primary debt to the Greeks? Simply the critical spirit" (249). Gilbert: "What are the unreal things, but the passions that once burned one like fire? What are the incredible things, but the things that one has faithfully believed? What are the improbable things? The things that one has done oneself" (270).

2. **Imagery:** Why does it seem so important for Wilde to use imagery in this work?

Wilde uses vivid language throughout *The Critic as Artist* in order to draw readers in and make them employ their senses: "It is well for our vanity that we slay the criminal, for if we suffered him to live he might show us what we had gained by his crime. It is well for his peace that the saint goes to his martyrdom. He is spared the sight of the horror of his harvest" (257). The unusual and fascinating thing about this particular passage is that Wilde mentions some of the senses, as if to make us aware of the effects of imagery, and also uses imagery, leaving us with a vivid picture and a rather shocked frame of mind.

Compare and Contrast Essays

Comparing and contrasting elements in a literary work is a very useful way of finding similarities and differences on which you can then comment. Do not simply make a list of similarities and/or differences and assume that you are finished. The purpose of comparisons and contrasts is to invoke the larger issues in the story, and in order to do that effectively the similarities and differences must not only be found, they must also be analyzed.

One of the most obvious elements of a text to compare and contrast is character. This is why the analysis is so important. Of course you will find similarities and differences between two characters in a literary work, just as you would find similarities and differences between any two people you know. So what? You must draw conclusions from those similarities and/ or differences. Often you will find that the most interesting analyses stem from the most unlikely comparisons. In this case, if you count Wilde, we have three characters available for comparison and contrast, but there are several options for other types of comparisons and contrasts.

Sample Topics:

1. **Journalism versus literature:** What was the general public's opinion of literature and journalism? Is it necessary to pit them against each other? Couldn't they work together?

   Ernest asks, "But what is the difference between literature and journalism?" and Gilbert quips, "Oh! journalism is unreadable and literature is not read" (248). But what really was the difference in Wilde's view? Some research on the practice and reception of journalism in the late 19th century will be helpful in writing a paper on this topic. Presumably Wilde would approve of literature long before finding himself in league with journalists. Yet Wilde's personality, fame, and career depended on journalism, and he participated in it, to some degree, when he wrote letters to various editors and published articles.

2. **Action versus writing:** Are acting and writing mutually exclusive? Are both the playgrounds of dreamers? Why does Wilde choose to differentiate between them this way?

   Gilbert says, "It is very much more difficult to talk about a thing than to do it. . . . Anybody can make history. Only a great man can write it" (256). It is relatively clear that without action, many writers would have nothing to record, and without writers, those making history would be quickly forgotten. Yet Gilbert clearly skims this mutual need and privileges writing above action. Why? Gilbert also says of action that "Its basis is the lack of imagination. It is the last resource of those who know not how to dream" (256). Immediately after making this comment, Gilbert seems to contradict himself: "the one person who has more illusions than the dreamer is the man of action" (256).

Bibliography for *The Critic as Artist*

Danson, Lawrence. "Wilde as Critic and Theorist." *Cambridge Companion to Oscar Wilde.* Ed. Peter Raby. Cambridge: Cambridge UP, 1997. 80–95.

Repplier, Agnes. "*Intentions* as year's 'best book'." 1892. *Oscar Wilde: The Critical Heritage.* Ed. Karl Beckson. New York: Barnes & Noble, 1970. 103–06.

Roditi, Edouard. *Oscar Wilde.* Norfolk: New Directions Books, 1947.

Unsigned review. 1891. *Oscar Wilde: The Critical Heritage.* Ed. Karl Beckson. NY: Barnes & Noble, 1970. 90–91.

Wilde, Oscar. *The Critic as Artist.* 1890. *Oscar Wilde: The Major Works.* Ed. Isobel Murray. Oxford: Oxford UP, 2000. 241–98.

DE PROFUNDIS

READING TO WRITE

ONE OF the crucial questions to ask about *De Profundis* is whether it should be considered a private letter or a public performance. Did Wilde really intend for only Bosie to read it? Did he write it in letter form because it was easiest or made the most sense, or did he want to make a particular point to or about Bosie? Did he plan to publish it all along? Part of the story behind *De Profundis* involves the restrictions on Wilde while in Reading prison. He could write, but it had to be turned in every evening and would not be given back to Wilde the next day. Richard Ellmann, Wilde's preeminent biographer, writes of Wilde's genius plan: "He would write a letter to Alfred Douglas ["Bosie"], as he was allowed to do by rule, but such a letter as would also offer an autobiographical account of his last five years. It would follow, like a parable, his progress from pleasure to pain and then, in the last months, to a change of heart and mastery of pain" (510). Even with this knowledge, we can read the book/letter and ask a number of questions about its inception, its intent, its creation, and its reception.

Much of the letter seems very personal, and yet there are sections where Wilde appears to be writing for a wider audience, making points about life and art in general, whether or not they relate directly to his relationship with Bosie. Look at the following paragraphs as an example of Wilde writing to a wider audience:

> I was a man who stood in symbolic relations to the art and culture of my age. I had realised this for myself at the very dawn of my manhood, and had forced my age to realise it afterwards. Few men hold such a position

in their own lifetime and have it so acknowledged. It is usually discerned, if discerned at all, by the historian, or the critic, long after both the man and his age have passed away. With me it was different. I felt it myself, and made others feel it. Byron was a symbolic figure, but his relations were to the passion of his age and its weariness of passion. Mine were to something more noble, more permanent, of more vital issue, of larger scope.

The gods had given me almost everything. I had genius, a distinguished name, high social position, brilliancy, intellectual daring: I made art a philosophy, and philosophy an art: I altered the minds of men and the colours of things: there was nothing I said or did that did not make people wonder: I took the drama, the most objective form known to art, and made it as personal a mode of expression as the lyric of the sonnet, at the same time that I widened its range and enriched its characterisation: drama, novel, poem in rhyme, poem in prose, subtle or fantastic dialogue, whatever I touched I made beautiful in a new mode of beauty: to truth itself I gave what is false no less than what is true as its rightful province, and showed that the false and the true are merely forms of intellectual existence. I treated Art as the supreme reality, and life as a mere mode of fiction: I awoke the imagination of my century so that it created myth and legend around me: I summed up all systems in a phrase, and all existence in an epigram. (57)

Certainly you could argue that in these paragraphs Wilde is simply trying to make himself better known to Bosie by explaining who he was before meeting Bosie and how he sees himself as an artist, a public figure, and a man. Yet you might also argue that the overall tone of this section lends itself better to a public readership, where his glory might resonate more profoundly.

However you argue about this section, there are further questions you can pursue: Is he overstating his importance as an artist, as a figure of his time, and as a figure beyond his time? In some ways this section reads as if Wilde has written his own eulogy and predicted what would be said about him long after his death. How much of his self-characterization and congratulation is accurate? What are his motivations for describing himself and his work in these ways? What message does it send to Bosie and other readers? Do these paragraphs help us to better understand Wilde's work in general and his attitudes toward them?

Does he sound regretful when he says, "I treated Art as the supreme reality, and life as a mere mode of fiction"? When interpreting *De Profundis* it is important to remain aware of Wilde's circumstances: his place in prison and his loss of his wife and children. How does that affect his writing, his ideas, and his perceptions of himself?

Reading one more paragraph offers even greater insight to Wilde's self-portrait:

> Along with these things, I had things that were different. I let myself be lured into long spells of senseless and sensual ease. I amused myself with being a *flâneur*, a dandy, a man of fashion. I surrounded myself with the smaller natures and the meaner minds. I became the spendthrift of my own genius, and to waste an eternal youth gave me a curious joy. Tired of being on the heights I deliberately went to the depths in the search for new sensations. What the paradox was to me in the sphere of thought, perversity became to me in the sphere of passion. Desire, at the end, was a malady, or a madness, or both. I grew careless in the lives of others. I took pleasure where it pleased me and passed on. I forgot that every little action of the common day makes or unmakes character, and that therefore what one has done in the secret chamber one has some day to cry aloud on the housetops. I ceased to be Lord over myself. I was no long the Captain of my Soul, and did not know it. I allowed you to dominate me, and your father to frighten me. I ended in horrible disgrace. There is only one thing for me now, absolute Humility: just as there is only one thing for you, absolute Humility also. You had better come down into the dust and learn it beside me. (58)

Is this Wilde's apology to his family, his friends, and himself? These paragraphs contain some of Wilde's most famous writing, such as "I became the spendthrift of my own genius." Pulled out of context such phrases (or aphorisms) seem witty and light. In context, however, they become sorrowful and somewhat reverent. Why would Wilde concern himself with such eloquence in writing if he were only expecting Bosie to read it?

A careful reading of the text will allow you to look for elements that interest you that might be drawn into larger questions, issues, patterns, and ideas. Familiarizing yourself with the text itself becomes very helpful when finding necessary evidence that supports the claims in your paper.

TOPICS AND STRATEGIES

This section of the chapter discusses various possible topics for essays on *De Profundis* and general approaches to these topics. Be aware that the material below is only a place to start from, not some kind of master key to the perfect essay. Use this material to prompt your own thinking. Every topic discussed here could encompass a wide variety of effective papers.

Themes

A theme is an idea or concept that helps to inform the plot and is often found by looking carefully for repeated words, phrases, and ideas in a work. When more than one character experiences the same or similar things, or when there is notable repetition of an action or an idea, you can bet that you have identified a theme. The next step is to ask what the work is saying about the theme. Do characters have differing opinions on it? Does the author seem to want readers to learn a particular lesson about this theme? In other words, your work is not done once you have identified a theme. The real heart of your paper lies in your analysis and interpretation of a theme.

De Profundis is unusual in this respect because we do not get various characters' voices here, in the traditional sense. We get Wilde's thoughts, feelings, and opinions alone. Yet we can look for themes in much the same way, thinking about ideas that he repeats and conveys with some sort of additional message. That message, in this case, is particularly complex. *De Profundis* is a deeply personal letter, but it is also a diatribe, a list of wrongs, a catalog of Wilde's own failings, and an indictment of Bosie and his parents. Perhaps part of figuring out a theme for this work is deciding whether you believe *De Profundis* to be a private letter or a public condemnation. Are there themes here that seem to pertain to Bosie in particular—things that Wilde specifically would have wanted Bosie to know? Are there themes that seem to aim at a wider audience— things that Wilde wanted to communicate to general readers or, more specifically, a late 19th-century audience?

Sample Topics:

1. Debt: Who owes what to whom and why?

It seems that everyone Wilde mentions in *De Profundis* has a debt to pay: "For every single thing that is done someone has to pay" (112). Some of the text (pages 29 and 41, for example) contain an actual itemization of expenses, and Wilde spends a lot of time making sure that Bosie understands the actual financial strain that Wilde has been under. What are some of the figurative or metaphoric debts in *De Profundis*? Does Bosie owe those to Wilde too, or does Wilde have his own debts to pay? Consider our language today and the way in which we refer to prisoners as "paying a debt to society." Is that what Wilde is doing? Is that a fair way to look at the prison system? How would Wilde answer these questions?

2. Love/hate: Do Wilde and Bosie have a classic love/hate relationship?

Always remember when writing about the relationship between Bosie and Wilde that *De Profundis* only gives us one side of the story. You might want to read *My Friendship with Oscar Wilde* or one of the other publications written by Lord Alfred ("Bosie") Douglas himself to get the other perspective. According to Wilde, there are clear lines to be drawn between love and hate, and Wilde professes himself on the side of love, while Bosie languishes under the influence of his father's hate (and his hatred for his father). Is Wilde trying to educate Bosie about love and hate, or is he simply reduced to name-calling tactics on these topics? Consider the tone and intent of the following excerpts: "The aim of Love is to love: no more, and no less . . . Is it beginning to dawn on you what Love is, and what is the nature of Love? It is not too late for you to learn, though to teach it to you I may have had to go to a convict's cell" (39); and, "Hate, you have yet to learn, is, intellectually considered, the Eternal Negation. Considered from the point of view of the emotions it is a form of Atrophy, and kills everything but itself" (36).

3. **Imagination:** What exactly does Wilde mean when he writes about imagination?

When Wilde writes about imagination, he is not necessarily refer-ring to a wonderful ability to daydream. In some ways, it seems that he means the opposite of what we understand imagination to be: "Remember that imagination is the quality that enables one to see things and people in their real as in their ideal rela-tions" (113). We usually think of imagination as a lovely ideal or something that in the 19th century was generally referred to as "fancy." Is Wilde showing us the darker side of imagination? How so? Wilde also makes several connections between Christ and imagination: "Philistinism being simply that side of man's nature that is not illumined by the imagination, he sees all the lovely influences of life as modes of Light: the imagination itself is the world-light" (85). What effect does such an association have on our reading? What effect might it have had on Bosie or general readers of Wilde's day?

4. **Shallowness:** Who is actually shallow in *De Profundis*?

Wilde was (and still is) accused of shallowness in his life and his writing. People thought he paid too much attention to his appearance, and some critics felt he did not pay enough atten-tion to his writing. Does Wilde's writing in *De Profundis* indi-cate an understanding of this vision people have of him? Does he appear to have changed into a less shallow man (particularly consider some of the sections where he discusses himself as a "deeper man"), or does he believe that he has been "deeper" all along and others just failed to pay enough attention? Several times throughout *De Profundis* Wilde repeats, "The supreme vice is shallowness" (4). Clearly this is a message he wants to get through loudly and clearly. Does his characterization of Bosie as shallow seem fair? Why or why not?

5. **Shame:** Wilde clearly wants Bosie to feel shame. Does Wilde feel shame too?

Wilde writes to Bosie, "Secretly you must think of yourself with a good deal of shame" (100). This statement can be read in several ways. Wilde might be noting that Bosie cannot help but feel shameful. His use of the word "must" allows another interpretation, one that gives Wilde an authoritative voice telling Bosie that he should feel shame. Indeed it seems as if much of *De Profundis* is directed at that exact aim. Does it appear that Wilde feels some shame as well? If so, is it justified? If not, why not? How can you tell?

Character

When studying characters, there are several angles to take. You might look at character development or what distinguishes one character from another. You might also investigate change in a character, noting when a character seems to evolve (or devolve) in some way. Along the same lines, you can choose to study a character who perhaps should change but does not. In this case you can ask yourself whether or not Wilde changes throughout the course of *De Profundis*. It seems as if his tone starts out rather harsh and cruel, mellows into something more meditative and even religious, and then returns, at least in some measure, to the harshness and cruelty of the beginning. Do these changes in tone reveal changes in Wilde's "character"? Do we understand Wilde as a character in this piece, or is he writing solely and straightforwardly, honestly, as himself? How can you tell?

This work is, of course, unusual in that there are no characters in the fictional sense. The people Wilde writes about are all real, and yet given the extreme circumstances under which *De Profundis* was written, it would be easy to understand how and why Wilde might exaggerate certain characteristics of some people.

It is always fascinating to study the ways in which a character is created. This requires you to look at specific words, phrases, settings, or moods that surround and help describe a character in order to see how Wilde helps readers form appropriate opinions of his characters.

Sample Topics:

1. **Wilde:** How does Wilde present himself in this book?

Of course, in reading *De Profundis* we only have Wilde's words from Wilde's perspective. In order to evaluate his accuracy, you will want to read other sources such as Richard Ellmann's biography *Oscar Wilde*. But even if you have only read *De Profundis* you can answer some questions in order to come up with viable paper topics. Does Wilde seem to be even trying to portray himself fairly, or is the language of his writing such that we cannot get past his bias toward himself?

2. **Bosie:** How is Bosie portrayed in the book?

In some ways the entire book is about Bosie's character. You might consult additional sources, such as Lord Alfred ("Bosie") Douglas's *My Friendship with Oscar Wilde*, to get a better idea of whether or not Wilde's portrayal is in fact accurate. Even without this outside information, you can study what you feel Wilde's intentions for *De Profundis* were. Does he want to portray Bosie fairly? Does he know that Bosie will recognize (and possibly forgive) Wilde's exaggerations? Is Wilde more concerned with looking like the good guy than with telling the truth? After the book/letter was written, Wilde wrote a letter to his friend Robbie Ross in which he complains about what he feels was the misuse of his money before and during his prison term, and he seems to revoke some of his nastier characterizations of Bosie: "I asked in one of my letters if Alfred Douglas had been directing these operations. I am sorry I did so. It was unjust. It was unjust to unfortunate Alfred Douglas. He once played dice with his father for my life, and lost. I don't think he would again do so" (*Letters* 543).

3. **Bosie's parents:** What kind of blame does Wilde place on them?

Reading *De Profundis* gives us a clear picture of Bosie as a mama's boy and Bosie's father as a ruthless tyrant. Bosie's mother seems afraid of both of them, according to Wilde. Why does Wilde bring them into the discussion in the first place? How might we expect Bosie to react to the comparisons Wilde makes, particularly between Bosie and his father?

4. **Wilde's wife and children:** How does Wilde portray his family in *De Profundis*?

Wilde mourns the loss of time with his children, which "always will remain to me a source of infinite distress, of infinite pain, of grief without end or limit" (55). He seems to have a great deal of respect for his wife, Constance: "Our friendship has always been a source of distress to her: not merely because she had never liked you personally, but because she saw how your continual companionship altered me" (17). Do his words conflict with his actions?

History and Context

Studying history and context always involves research, and you can begin by choosing a character, a scene, a theme, or a setting from the work and enquiring as to whether that is what things were really like. Be aware that sometimes the time period in which the action of the work takes place can be different from the time in which the work was written and published, and even the difference of a few years can make a big difference. Once you have determined the similarities and differences between the real world and the Wildean one, you can begin to speculate about what Wilde is trying to convey through his portrayal.

History and context might also pertain to the author's biography, which in terms of *De Profundis* is absolutely crucial to understanding the work. Wilde fills readers in on many of the details of his life, particularly those pertaining to his trials and imprisonment. But in order to fully understand and appreciate his tone, you will want to read less-biased biographical information. Then perhaps you will be able to tell, for example, when Wilde is exaggerating.

Sample Topics:

1. **Bosie's response:** What did Bosie do with the information in the letter?

Did he read the letter? Did he read it as a letter or as a published "tract"? Did he respond? Look at his publications, including *Oscar Wilde and Myself* as well as his *Autobiography.* How do you think Wilde expected Bosie to respond? How did England respond to both Wilde and Bosie, particularly after Wilde's death?

2. **Publication of *De Profundis*:** What does anyone know for sure about Wilde's intentions?

Robbie Ross, Wilde's friend and literary executor, published an abridged version of *De Profundis* in 1905. To try to save Bosie's feelings, he did not reveal that it was written as a letter to Bosie, nor did he include Bosie's name or some of the details of Bosie's relationship with Wilde. Still, Bosie's involvement was clear. Eventually the full version of *De Profundis* was published, and Bosie fairly quickly published *Oscar Wilde and Myself.* "Douglas disclaimed [that] book later," and by the time he wrote his *Autobiography* in the late 1920s, "He tried to achieve detachment and forgiveness" (Ellmann 587).

Philosophy and Ideas

Writing about the philosophy and ideas found in a text is similar to writing about the text's theme, except that philosophy and ideas are applied more generally and live in some sense outside of the text, as well. So when writing about a book's philosophy and ideas, you are looking for the ways in which the work comments on general, often universal, ideas.

De Profundis is packed with Wilde's philosophies and ideas. Did he have these same ideas all of his life, or did they stem mainly from his trials and prison experience? Does Wilde's time in prison seem to have affected his views of the world? Do you think he is closer to finding life's truths because of his forced seclusion in prison, or is he living in a philosophical fantasy world?

Wilde always had something to say about art. Are his philosophies of art in *De Profundis* changed significantly from his earlier writings? What might account for changes? If there are no changes, why not? Some scholars have observed that the philosophies in *De Profundis* seem most closely related to *The Picture of Dorian Gray,* so reading both works and comparing and contrasting their philosophies might be a worthwhile endeavor.

Sample Topics:

1. **Art:** What does *De Profundis* reveal about Wilde's perceptions of art?

   Wilde has much to say about art in *De Profundis* and seems to be hoping and expecting his own art in writing to evolve as a result of his life experiences: "Perhaps there may come into my art also, no less than into my life, a still deeper note, one of greater unity of passion, and directness of impulse. Not width but intensity is the true aim of modern Art. We are no longer in Art concerned with the type. It is with the exception we have to do" (89). How does Wilde define art in *De Profundis*? Does the book/letter fit into his own definition of the term? Why or why not?

2. **Individualism:** How does Wilde define individualism?

   In *De Profundis* Wilde writes about the evolution of his character while in prison: "I am far more of an individualist than I ever was. Nothing seems to me of the smallest value except what one gets out of oneself" (59). Does Wilde's quest for individualism undermine Bosie's ability to achieve individualism on his own? In other words, if Wilde has to tell Bosie to become an individual, or educate him on becoming one, does it count? What do we make of the associations Wilde makes when he writes that "Christ is the most supreme of Individualists" (75)?

3. **Education:** Who is Wilde intending to educate with *De Profundis*?

   Think of the number of times Wilde uses the word "should" in this work. Clearly he sees himself as Bosie's instructor to some degree, and yet "Wilde was well aware . . . that [Bosie] would be impenetrable to moral persuasion, but for the sake of his own sanity and self-respect he felt he must make the effort" (Ellmann 512). Are there clues in the text showing that Wilde believed his attempts at educating Bosie were in vain? Which points/ideas does Wilde seem most interested in educating Bosie about?

Form and Genre

Form and genre provide ways of classifying works that usually allow us to study them more fully. Form is defined as the style and structure of a work, whereas genre is the type, or classification, of a work. Both form and genre are usually distinct from a work's content, though writers use each of them quite specifically in order to convey a particular message, reach a certain audience, or to simply strengthen the impact of their work.

Determining form and genre gives us one of the stickiest questions regarding *De Profundis*. What were Wilde's intentions here? He wrote it while in prison, and each day the guard would take Wilde's work away. The next day the guard brought new paper, but Wilde rarely got a chance to look back upon his previous writing. How do these facts about the writing process affect the form and genre of the work? Are there other works, by Wilde or anyone, comparable in form or genre to *De Profundis*?

Sample Topics:

1. **Intertextuality:** What effect do Wilde's references to other writers have?

   Intertextuality occurs when a work's meaning is shaped by other works/texts. Wilde mentions and/or quotes eminent scholars and artists such as Wordsworth, Pater, Shakespeare, Dante, Goethe, Carlyle, Arnold, Emerson, Baudelaire, and Keats. Is a reader of *De Profundis* required to have knowledge about those other writers in order to fully understand Wilde's work? What does this intertextuality reveal about Wilde's expectations of his reader(s)?

2. **Paradox:** In what ways does *De Profundis* both contain and create paradoxes?

   Wilde's writing in *De Profundis* contains paradoxes, certainly, but in some ways the entire piece is its own paradox as well. His intuition seems to be telling him that Bosie is a bad person and that they certainly do not belong together, yet the end of the letter seems to indicate that their relationship still has the potential for triumphing over all of this adversity. Why would he spend all of this time and energy writing presumably to demonstrate that Bosie is unworthy of his love, money, and time, only to turn around and practically beg Bosie to respond to the letter and meet him again? Consider "to Love all things are easy" (116) and "your absolute trust that I would always forgive you being the thing in you that I always liked the best, perhaps the best thing in you to like" (21).

3. **Letter:** Did Wilde intend this as a private letter or as a public document/publication? How can you tell?

A lot of *De Profundis* is rather vehemently focused on Bosie, but there are certainly parts of it that focus on Wilde, where we can see his transformation and learning process during his prison experience. Does all of it fit together, or do some parts seem like an interruption to the letter? Why do you think Wilde wrote this as a letter rather than a story or an essay? Did he have psychological reasons for doing so?

Language, Symbols, and Imagery

Writing about the language, symbols, and imagery within a work require you to look specifically at how the work is constructed, as opposed to just studying the content. Pay particular attention to words, phrases, and repetition of words, phrases and ideas in order to begin to see how Wilde uses language, symbols, and imagery. Summarizing the content may be necessary for illustrating particular points, but it is not the end product of this type of paper. You will want to look at things like syntax, word choice, and general diction. Ultimately, you are looking at Wilde's choices as a writer and the possible reasons behind his choices.

Finding symbolism in a work involves looking for something that stands for something else. These things might be tangible objects like letters or particular foods, but they might also be something like a particular color associated with similar things throughout the book. The best symbols represent more than one thing, so do not limit yourself to finding symbolism only in things that stand for one other thing.

An additionally intriguing aspect of *De Profundis* is that Wilde comments on language, symbols, and imagery even as he uses them as writing techniques. What does Wilde write about symbolism, for example? Does he practice what he preaches?

Imagery encapsulates things that can be perceived with our five senses: sight, sound, taste, smell, and touch. Which of our senses is Wilde trying to evoke in this work? Why? Can our reactions be presumed to be vastly different from those of Bosie, Robbie Ross, and other readers who were actually involved in Wilde's life? Why or why not?

Sample Topics:

1. **Repetition:** What effects does Wilde's repetition have on readers?

   Perhaps the most notable repeated sentences in *De Profundis* are: "The supreme vice is shallowness. Whatever is realised is right" (4, 35, 40, 113). Why does Wilde feel the need to highlight this particular point multiple times? Does the meaning behind it change in each particular context? What other words, phrases, and ideas does Wilde repeat? Why? Keep in mind the historical context. While Wilde is writing in prison, his work is taken from him each night and only occasionally returned to him, so perhaps some of the repetition is unintentional. Yet he did revise the entire work eventually, so it is still worth looking at these repeated words, phrases, and ideas.

2. **Aphorisms:** How can we tell if and when Wilde is being sincere when he so often reverts to the pithy, memorable, quotable phrase?

   "The fatal errors of life are not due to man's being unreasonable: an unreasonable moment may be one's finest moment. They are due to man's being logical. There is a wide difference" (32). "Whatever happens to another happens to oneself" (72). This is a type of writing for which Wilde was well-known. He has an ability to condense thoughts into a pithy, meaningful, and sometimes witty phrase. It is the 19th-century equivalent to today's soundbites, when a person being interviewed on TV is able to state their main point in a very succinct way. What effect do these aphorisms have on your reading of *De Profundis*? Do they make the writing seem even more profound, or do they distract from the overall emotion of the text by boiling things down to oversimplified comments?

3. **Metaphor/simile:** Is *De Profundis* itself one giant metaphor?

Wilde uses metaphor and simile quite liberally in this text. For example: "as though my life, whatever it had seemed to myself and others, had all the while been a real Symphony of Sorrow, passing through its rhythmically-linked movements to its certain resolution, with that inevitableness that in Art characterizes the treatment of every great theme" (19). What effect do these literary techniques have on readers? What effect does it seem that Wilde was trying to have?

4. **Symbolism:** Wilde uses symbolism in his work, and he also comments extensively on the use of symbols in literature as well as life.

Wilde writes about symbols quite a bit in *De Profundis*. He writes of Bosie's calling himself "Prince Fleur-de-Lys," which may inspire you to research that particular symbol for evidence of why Bosie would choose such a thing to represent himself. Wilde discusses symbols in more profound, almost philosophical ways as well: "the little things in life are symbols. We receive our bitter lessons most easily through them. Your seemingly casual choice of a feigned name was, and will remain, symbolic. It reveals you" (42). What is Wilde trying to say in this passage? What does the fleur-de-lys mean to him exactly? Why does he say that people learn lessons "most easily" through symbols? What consequence does such an idea have on the significance of literature to society?

5. **Untranslated languages:** Why does Wilde include so many words and phrases from other languages?

Many of the words and passages in languages besides English remain unexplained in the text and in the notes. Why? What does this reveal about Wilde's expectations for his reader's (or readers') knowledge base and education? What does this reveal about Wilde's own education and self-perception?

Compare and Contrast Essays

Writing a paper that compares and/or contrasts elements of the work involves much more than simply listing similarities and differences between two or more things. These lists might help you early in the drafting process, but your paper eventually needs to go beyond this point to discuss why these similarities and/or differences are notable and important to the work. You would do well to ask questions like: Does Wilde intentionally set up some comparisons in order to perhaps show different points of view or circumstances? Do we notice particular comparisons and contrasts simply because of the time in which we live and our perceptions of the 20th century?

One of the most interesting things you can do with this type of paper is to make a comparison between two or more things/characters that on the surface seem very similar. The more surprising your comparison or contrast is, the more engaging your paper could be to your readers (provided you back yourself up with sufficient evidence from the text). You cannot make a comparison or contrast statement based solely on your own perceptions and "feelings" about the work. Whatever claim you decide to make must be supportable through the text itself.

Sample Topics:

1. **Sins of the flesh and sins of the soul:** Are there degrees of sin, according to Wilde?

   There is a clear delineation for Wilde when it comes to a discussion of sin: "Sins of the flesh are nothing. . . . Sins of the soul alone are shameful" (39). What exactly is the distinction he is trying to make, and why is it so important for him to make it?

2. **A better man and a deeper man:** What is the difference?

Wilde writes, "while to propose to be a better man is a piece of unscientific cant, to have become a *deeper* man is the privilege of those who have suffered. And such I think I have become. You can judge for yourself" (88). What does it seem to mean to Wilde to be a better man versus a deeper man? Think of "deeper man" particularly in light of his accusations about Bosie's shallowness.

3. **Bosie and Wilde:** Are they really more alike than they are different from one another?

Wilde certainly spends virtually the entire letter differentiating between himself and Bosie. Can you pinpoint places, though, where Wilde and Bosie seem more alike than they are different? Is Wilde, in other words, guilty of some of the things he accuses Bosie of being or doing? For example, in the third paragraph of *De Profundis*, Wilde proposes that Bosie "read the letter over and over again till it kills [Bosie's] vanity" (3). But when Wilde attacks Bosie's "lack of any real appreciation of [his] genius," doesn't that reveal Wilde's vanity (107)?

Bibliography for *De Profundis*

Ellmann, Richard. *Oscar Wilde.* New York: Vintage Books, 1988.

Wilde, Oscar. *De Profundis.* 1897. New York: Modern Library, 2000.

———. *The Letters of Oscar Wilde.* Ed. Rupert Hart-Davis. New York: Harcourt, Brace and World, 1962.

THE DECAY OF LYING

READING TO WRITE

THERE ARE several pertinent questions to ask while reading *The Decay of Lying*. Is Wilde really promoting lying? If so, why? If not, why does he make it sound that way? Was Wilde a liar himself? In what capacity? Can we trust him as a writer? What kinds of clues does he give in the text to indicate when he is lying and when he is being sincere and truthful? Why does he use his own sons' names in this dialogue? Wilde's son Vyvyan writes, "Particularly did I like *The Decay of Lying*, which I read over and over again. There were my brother's name and my own set out for all to see" (Holland 179).

The liar in *The Decay of Lying* seems to be modeled on Wilde himself. A friend of his said, "Romantic imagination was strong in him, but there was always something in his telling of . . . tale[s] to suggest that he felt his hearers were not really being taken in" (Nunokawa 10). Did Wilde *want* his hearers to be taken in? Perhaps Wilde pinpoints his own complexity with the simple question "who wants to be consistent?" (*Decay* 216). The only thing we seem to know for sure about Wilde's feelings toward his writing here is that he wanted to get attention: "I have blown my trumpet against the gate of dullness" (*Letters* 237). His idea certainly worked in that capacity. An unsigned review from the June 6, 1891, *Athenaeum* calls Wilde "a contributor of something fresh, something original and stimulating, amongst the mass of matter about art that has been written during the last twenty years."

Studying one passage of the work carefully can generate several ideas for further investigation:

VIVIAN. My dear fellow, whatever you may say, it is merely a dramatic utterance, and no more represents Shakespeare's real views upon art than the speeches of Iago represent his real views upon morals. But let me get to the end of the passage:

"Art finds her own perfection within, and not outside of, herself. She is not to be judged by any external standard of resemblance. She is a veil, rather than a mirror. She has flowers that no forests know of, birds that no woodland possesses. She makes and unmakes many worlds, and can draw the moon from heaven with a scarlet thread. Hers are the "forms more real than living man", and hers the great archetypes of which things that have existence are but unfinished copies. Nature has, in her eyes, no laws, no uniformity. She can work miracles at her will, and when she calls monsters from the deep they come. She can bid the almond tree blossom in winter, and send the snow upon the ripe corn-field. At her word the frost lays its silver finger on the burning mouth of June, and the winged lions creep out from the hollows of the Lydian hills. The dryads peer from the thicket as she passes by, and the brown fauns smile strangely at her when she comes near them. She has hawk-faced gods that worship her, and the centaurs gallop at her side."

CYRIL. I like that. I can see it. Is that the end?

VIVIAN. No. There is one more passage, but it is purely practical. It simply suggests some methods by which we could revive this lost art of Lying.

CYRIL. Well, before you read it to me, I should like to ask you a question. What do you mean by saying that life, 'poor, probable, uninteresting human life', will try to reproduce the marvels of art? I can quite understand your objection to art being treated as a mirror. You think it would reduce genius to the position of a cracked looking-glass. But you don't mean to say that you seriously believe that Life imitates Art, that Life in fact is the mirror, and Art the reality? (*Decay*, 228)

One of the first questions a reader might pursue concerns Vivian's mention of Shakespeare's Iago. Is Wilde really writing of himself here, asking readers to note that *The Decay of Lying*, too, is a "dramatic utterance," and Wilde himself may not share the feelings and opinions of his characters? Certainly Wilde believed in the power of words that Vivian speaks of, and he also believed that life imitates art, at least to some extent.

You might also look at this passage for Wilde's writing techniques. He uses quite a bit of imagery in Vivian's description of Nature, which Cyril acknowledges by saying, "I can see it." What effect does Wilde's imagery have? Does it help him make some of his more philosophical points in some way?

Finally, you might ask questions about the characters themselves. Look at the very end of this passage. Does Cyril voice an opinion there? Is Cyril speaking on behalf of the readers? Why or why not? How can you tell? Why is Vivian reading his own article aloud? What is the affect of this on Cyril? On readers?

TOPICS AND STRATEGIES

This section of the chapter addresses various possible topics for writing about *The Decay of Lying* as well as general methods for approaching these topics. These lists are in no way exhaustive and are meant to provide a jumping-off point rather than an answer key. Use these suggestions to find your own ideas and form your own analyses. All topics discussed in this chapter could turn into very effective papers.

Themes

A theme in a literary work is an idea, an action, an occurrence, or a system that in some way threads itself throughout the work. Themes are often identifiable through a close reading of words, phrases, and ideas, and they are recognizable as something about which the character(s) and/or author appear to have much to say. In other words, if a work's action and/or characters continually return to a similar idea, you have probably identified a theme of the book. Remember though, it is not enough to simply identify a theme. Writing about a work's theme also involves determining the purpose, or influence, of the theme in the work. Why would Wilde focus on defining art, for example? How does this particular theme help us to identify specific parts of Wilde's intended audience? Does this theme relate to anything similar in Wilde's other works?

Wilde wrote that *The Decay of Lying* contained his "new views on art, and particularly on the relations of art and history" (*Letters* 236). Is Wilde's statement on art actually the main point of *The Decay of Lying*? Why or why not? How can you tell?

Sample Topics:

1. **Definitions of art:** Which definition of art does *The Decay of Lying* seem to promote?

   Wilde discusses and defines art many times in this piece: "Art begins with abstract decoration with purely imaginative and pleasurable work dealing with what is unreal and non-existent" (224); "Art itself is really a form of exaggeration; and selection, which is the very spirit of art, is nothing more than an intensified mode of over-emphasis" (224); "Art finds her own perfection within, and not outside of, herself. She is not to be judged by any external standard of resemblance. She is a veil, rather than a mirror" (228). Do all of these definitions and descriptions tie together, or is the point rather to fragment readers' views of art, so that it can no longer be clearly defined or boxed in?

2. **Lying:** Is Wilde advocating lying in all circumstances? Are there degrees of lying that are acceptable or unacceptable?

   Is all lying acceptable as long as it is for the purpose of art? Vivian claims in *The Decay of Lying* that "Truth is entirely and absolutely a matter of style" (227). Wilde (as Vivian) provides several forms: "Lying for the sake of gaining some immediate personal advantage" (237), "Lying for the sake of the improvement of the young" (237), "Lying for the sake of a monthly salary" (238), but "The only form of lying that is absolutely beyond reproach is Lying for its own sake, and the highest development of this is . . . Lying in Art" (238). In other words, "Lying, the telling of beautiful untrue things, is the proper aim of Art" (239). Clearly Wilde is not just writing about fiction here. What are the nuances of his arguments about lying?

Character

The most obvious fact about *The Decay of Lying* is that it contains characters, as opposed to the more straightforward, author's-point-of-view essay we might expect. Why does Wilde choose to use characters in this piece? Is he hiding behind them? Is he using them to express views other than his own? If so, what is his overall purpose for the essay? Is Wilde simply trying to keep the essay entertaining by introducing characters that actually speak for him? Is he practicing dialogue writing for future plays?

The Decay of Lying does not offer the kinds of character arcs we usually see in novels or plays. We do not see Cyril or Vivian in a very particular setting, we do not see them interact with anyone but each other, and we do not see significant character growth or change from beginning to end. Why then, would Wilde even bother to use characters? Is there any sort of development for Cyril and/or Vivian throughout the essay? Do the characters overshadow the points Wilde is trying to make about art? In an essay in support of lying, how can believe anything the characters and writer say?

Why does Wilde name the characters after his sons, who at the time *The Decay of Lying* was written were three and a half and two years old? Can Cyril and Vivian even be called characters in the truest literary sense? Are Cyril and Vivian caricatures, or do they develop some depth?

At certain points Wilde seems to be trying to make Cyril and Vivian a bit ridiculous. For example, the section near the end about nature imitating art becomes a bit lopsided. This, soon after Vivian has declared, "I am prepared to prove anything" (232). Is he really? Are we rather to believe that Vivian's arguments are not all completely thought through, that he is "prepared to prove anything" only to the degree that he likes to discuss and argue and is ready to pull an argument (or "proof") out of the air in order to try to influence others' opinions?

Sample Topics:

1. **Cyril:** What is Cyril's role here?

> Does Cyril represent the majority of readers? If so, how can you tell? Why does he interrupt or interject at those particular times? Why does he have little to say through most of the piece but more to share regarding mirrors, for example? Does

Cyril largely agree or disagree with Vivian? Why? How can you tell? What effect of influence does Wilde seem to want Cyril to have on readers? Use evidence from the text to support your points. Does Wilde set him up as the less-knowledgeable one who needs to be persuaded? Why might this dynamic be useful or necessary for Wilde's purpose?

2. **Vivian:** Is Vivian a stand-in or mouthpiece for Wilde?

Where do his opinions come together and/or diverge from Wilde's? How can we tell? Would Wilde's 19th-century audience have known what Wilde's real opinions were? Does anyone, even today, know Wilde's true opinions? Vivian tells Cyril that he is writing an article called "The Decay of Lying: A Protest" (216). Wilde's piece is actually titled *The Decay of Lying: An Observation.* What do the slight differences between the titles reveal about both Vivian and Wilde? Do they share the same intentions for their writing? Wilde writes, "it is merely a dramatic utterance, and no more represents Shakespeare's real views upon art than the speeches of Iago represent his real views upon morals" (228). These words come from Vivian, which seems to indicate that Wilde is making a warning about conflating an author's thoughts with his character's words.

History and Context

Studying the history and context of a work allows you to address the background of either (or both) the work and the author. Wilde often uses his work as a critique of 19th-century England, making investigations into the Victorian period extremely useful.

The Decay of Lying has virtually no setting, no detail other than the characters' names and the small place detail of "the library of a country house in Nottinghamshire" (215). Yet the piece has much to tell readers about its history and context. What does the work uncover about Victorian thought and feeling, particularly regarding art and lying? What do we learn about Wilde himself through this piece?

Learning about the background of even the smallest detail mentioned in a literary work can provide greater insight into characters, plot, and, of course, setting. For a paper focusing on history and context, you might look at general attitudes and behaviors that characters share. This type of background information will help you to form a thesis about a particular character's actions (or nonactions), about the accuracy of Wilde's settings, and even sometimes about Wilde's opinions of the events and ideologies of his time.

Sample Topics:

1. **Name-dropping:** What do these names tell us about the 1889 audience for whom Wilde is writing?

Wilde mentions dozens of names in this piece: Morris, Wordsworth, Stevenson, James, Oliphant, Zola, Ruskin, Eliot, and many more. Why does he discuss so many different people in this essay? What if anything do the people have in common? What kind of footnotes or additional research do these names require from today's readers? Is it important to know who all of these people are, or can we get Wilde's point just from the larger context? Why does Wilde seem to be lumping some names together? How can we tell when his criticisms are serious and when they are sarcastic or tongue-in-cheek?

2. **Responses to criticism:** Several places in the text contain Wilde's responses, sometimes couched and sometimes blatant, to criticisms of his life and work. For example, when he writes that the modern novelist "has not even the courage of other people's ideas" (217), he is clearly echoing a phrase used by James McNeill Whistler, who accused Wilde of plagiarism: "Oscar . . . has the courage of the opinions . . . of others" (Whistler 164).

Philosophy and Ideas

Writing about the philosophy and ideas found in a text is similar to writing about the text's theme, except that philosophy and ideas are applied more generally and live in some sense outside of the text as well. So when writing about a work's philosophy and ideas, you are looking for the ways in which the work comments on general ideas.

In what ways do Wilde's philosophies and ideas in *The Decay of Lying* relate to his ideas in some of his other works? For example, Wilde addresses hedonism on some level in *The Picture of Dorian Gray*. Do his views on the subject seem to change between the two works? Why are these similarities or differences significant?

It is often very difficult to tell when Wilde is writing seriously and when he is writing tongue in cheek or sarcastically. How do you think Wilde really feels about lying? Does he lie to readers in *The Decay of Lying*? How can you tell?

Sample Topics:

1. **Hedonism:** Is Wilde encouraging hedonism or is he making fun of it—or both?

    Vivian says that "the aim of the liar is simply to charm, to delight, to give pleasure" (227). This follows the hedonist way of life fairly closely—pleasure is the most important goal. Yet Wilde seems to be using *The Decay of Lying* in order to criticize hedonists as well. Who are "The Tired Hedonists" really (217)?

2. **Life imitates art:** Is Wilde able to prove that life actually does imitate art?

    There were a few times in Wilde's life when he seemed to be making a particular point to make his life imitate his art. Did this only work for him when he was doing it deliberately, or is life imitating art a natural occurrence? Wilde writes, "A great artist invents a type, and Life tries to copy it, to reproduce it in a popular form" (229). Did anyone try to copy the "types" in Wilde's work? Why or why not? How does this help prove Wilde's point that life does in fact imitate art? Wilde also writes that "Life is Art's best, Art's only pupil" (229). What does Wilde learn from art in his own life? How can you tell?

3. **Nature imitates art:** Is Wilde able to maintain this argument throughout *The Decay of Lying*?

    Vivian says that "Nature is no great mother who has borne us. She is our creation. It is in our brain that she quickens to life. Things are because we see them, and what we see, and how we see it, depends on the Arts that have influenced us" (233). Is this where the argument falls apart? "External Nature also imitates Art. The only effects that she can show us are effects that we have already seen through poetry, or in paintings. This is the secret of Nature's charm, as well as the explanation of Nature's weakness" (239). To what extent does this become a chicken-and-egg argument? If art came first, then what inspired it, and how did "external Nature" come to be? Is the argument meant to be that literal, or is Wilde's larger argument about point of view and the extreme ways in which art is able to influence our perceptions? In his letters, Wilde wrote, "The highest art is for our service, as the grandest nature is for her own service" (*Letters* 240).

4. Lying: Is Wilde lying in *The Decay of Lying*? Does it matter?

If it is truly art, isn't it supposed to be a lie? Wilde scholar Epifanio San Juan, Jr., claims that in this article Wilde gives us "a transvaluation of values. Given a new context, 'lying' denotes 'an accurate description of what has never occurred.' Like 'lying', the word 'insincerity' assumes a new reference: it becomes 'a method by which we can multiply our personalities'" (7).

Form and Genre

Form and genre provide ways of classifying works that usually allow us to study them more fully. Form is defined as the style and structure of a work, whereas genre is the type, or classification, of a work. Both form and genre are usually distinct from a work's content, though writers use each of them quite specifically in order to convey a particular message, reach a certain audience, or to simply strengthen the impact of their work. *The Decay of Lying* is written as a critical dialogue rather than a straightforward essay or a more acceptably creative form like a play or novel. Studying the form of the piece and Wilde's intentions for it can provide great insight into both the work and the writer.

Wilde wrote of *The Decay of Lying*, "It is meant to bewilder the masses by its fantastic form; *au fond* it is of course serious" (*Letters* 236). Wilde boasted that he did not want the "vulgarizing" public to understand his views on art, so he wrote about them in a form that would keep them from even trying. So the question becomes, why bother writing (and especially publishing) these views in the first place? Did Wilde really set out to "bewilder" people, or is that an excuse or a response to criticism?

He wrote the above comment in an 1889 letter, after the first publication of *The Decay of Lying* but before revising the piece. Implications? Do his revisions indicate a desire to be better understood by the masses, or does he seem to try even harder to confuse readers? Why? How can you tell? In another letter Wilde wrote, "underneath the fanciful form it hides some truths, or perhaps some half-truths, about art, which I think require to be put forward" (*Letters* 237). Clearly, he did want at least some of his ideas to be understood.

Sample Topics:

1. **Critical dialogue:** Is the dialogue between Vivian and Cyril more effective than a straightforward essay or a more "artful" play or novel?

   In many ways the form of *The Decay of Lying* gives readers more obstacles to overcome. Are Cyril and Vivian real in any sense of the word? Do they represent Wilde or other actual people? If Wilde had written this piece as a simple essay, we could have understood the ideas in it to be his. In the critical dialogue form, the ideas are conveyed as Cyril's or Vivian's, and readers need to discover for themselves the extent to which Wilde's actual feelings and ideas hide behind these characters.

2. **Realism:** Does Wilde use realism at any point in the essay?

   Realism is "literal-minded fidelity to social surfaces" (Kiberd 283). Think of a documentary, or a more journalistic piece, and you have a sense of realism. In some ways *The Decay of Lying* takes place in a vacuum, with very little detail as to the setting and characterizations. Are there any depictions of everyday life in the piece? Does Wilde seem to believe Vivian, who says, "As a method, realism is a complete failure?" (225). Is it possible to avoid realism entirely? Wilde writes much about masks and disguises: "In Wilde's terms, only the unique individual . . . , a creator not a product, is fully human. You have to be artificial to be yourself" (Danson 87). Is Wilde able to apply his theories and criticisms of realism to his writing in *The Decay of Lying*?

Language, Symbols, and Imagery

Hesketh Pearson writes that Wilde's dialogues "catch the accents of a real talker . . . their matter is as invigorating as their manner is fresh" (x). Writing about the language, symbols, and imagery in literature requires you to look specifically at how the work is constructed, as opposed to just studying the content of the work. Pay particular attention to words, phrases, and repetition of words, phrases, and ideas in order to begin to see how Wilde uses language, symbols, and imagery. Summarizing the content may be necessary for illustrating particular points, but it is not the end product of this type of paper. You will want to look at things like syntax, word choice, and general diction. Do Vivian and Cyril speak differently from one another? If so, why? Speech can be tied to all kinds of issues like economic class, education, geography, and stress, just to name a few. Discovering that two characters have distinct ways of speaking might lead you to research on economic classes and their respective educations, requiring some background in the historical context. Ultimately, you are looking at Wilde's choices as a writer and the possible reasons behind such choices.

Finding symbolism in a work involves looking for something that stands for something else. Is lying really just telling a fib in *The Decay of Lying*, or does lying stand for something else, like the revolt against stifling social stereotypes?

Imagery encapsulates things that can be perceived with our five senses: sight, sound, taste, smell, and touch.

Sample Topics:

1. **Humor:** How can we tell when Wilde is using humor to make a point?

   Why does he use humor in some parts of this piece? What effect would this humor have had on late 19th-century readers? What effect does it have on readers today? Why?

2. **Irony:** Which points does Wilde make by using irony? Why?

> Irony is the discrepancy between actual and expected results.
> Vivian talks about the story of George Washington and the
> cherry tree, and how Americans revere the man because he was
> incapable of telling a lie. Then Vivian claims that "The story of
> the cherry-tree is an absolute myth" (226). The idea that Ameri-
> cans' respect for a man who supposedly could not lie is based on
> a lie is ironic, to say the least. What does this instance of irony
> reveal about Vivian's (and perhaps Wilde's) thoughts and ideas
> on the matter?

Compare and Contrast Essays

It is usually easy to find elements of a literary work to hold up for comparison and/or contrast. It is considerably more challenging (and therefore more rewarding) to not only point out similarities and differences
between characters or elements in the work but to investigate why those
similarities and differences are important to the literature.

Comparisons and contrasts are often more interesting and fun if the
pairing is unexpected. Be sure to consider the larger questions involved
in your comparison and/or contrast. What effect does such a pairing/
grouping have on the work as a whole, on readers' responses to the work,
on the writer's apparent intentions for the work, etc.?

Sample Topics:

1. **Unimaginative realism and imaginative reality:** What is the
   difference, really?

   > Unimaginative realism is, presumably, a writer's attempt to
   > write realism that somehow fails because it contains no imagi-
   > nation. One could say that writers like Wilde and Dickens are
   > successful because they include elements of their world in their
   > writing, but they allow their imaginations to create the scene,
   > theme, etc. So imaginative reality is the "real world" dealt with
   > in particularly imaginative ways, for which Wilde's own life
   > seems to be one of the best examples. When he brings up these
   > two ideas, is Wilde comparing art/writing with life? Does he

see them as more similar than they are different? Why or why not? How can you tell?

2. **Cyril and Vivian:** Are they the same person (personality) in some ways?

What are the key differences between Cyril and Vivian in *The Decay of Lying*? Do you think Wilde intended them to be distinct "characters," or does he want them to appear fairly interchangeable? Do they both represent Wilde himself, or does one of them seem more like Wilde than the other?

Bibliography for *The Decay of Lying*

Danson, Lawrence. "Wilde as Critic & Theorist." *Cambridge Companion to Oscar Wilde.* Ed. Peter Raby. Cambridge: Cambridge UP, 1997. 80–95.

Kiberd, Declan. "Oscar Wilde: The Resurgence of Lying." *Cambridge Companion to Oscar Wilde.* Ed. Peter Raby. Cambridge: Cambridge UP, 1997. 276–94.

Holland, Vyvyane. *Son of Oscar Wilde.* London: Rupert Hart-Davis, 1954.

Nunokawa, Jeff, and Amy Sickels. *Oscar Wilde.* Gay and Lesbian Writers Series. Lesléa Newman, series editor. Philadelphia: Chelsea House, 2005.

Pearson, Hesketh. Introduction. *Essays by Oscar Wilde.* Freeport, NY: Books for Libraries Press, 1950. vii–xiii.

San Juan, Epifanio, Jr. *The Art of Oscar Wilde.* Princeton, NJ: Princeton UP, 1967.

Whistler, James McNeill. *The Gentle Art of Making Enemies.* New York: Putnam's, 1906.

Wilde, Oscar. *The Decay of Lying.* 1891. *Oscar Wilde: The Major Works.* Oxford: Oxford UP, 2000. 215–40.

———. *The Letters of Oscar Wilde.* Ed. Rupert Hart-Davis. New York: Harcourt, Brace and World, 1962.

THE PICTURE OF DORIAN GRAY

READING TO WRITE

*T*HE *PICTURE OF DORIAN GRAY* is Oscar Wilde's only novel, and it remains one of his best-known works. It is a unique book, not only because of the way it is written and its treatment of its subject matter, but because Wilde had a lot to say about it, and because English society and the courts had a lot to say about it too.

Wilde summed up *The Picture of Dorian Gray* in a number of different ways, making it a fascinating study and a great possible paper topic to compare his own conceptions of his work. At one point Wilde wrote: "My story is an essay on decorative art. It reacts against the crude brutality of plain realism. It is poisonous if you like, but you cannot deny that it is also perfect, and perfection is what we artist aim at" (*Letters* 264). What does Wilde mean when he calls the work "perfect"? Did readers of his own time have the same impression of the novel? Do readers today regard it as perfect? Why or why not?

The greatest irony surrounding this novel is that even while Wilde claimed to have written a complete invention, far from, as he puts it, "the crude brutality of plain realism," the novel was used as evidence in his trial. The conflation of the novel with reality was made complete when prosecuting attorneys condemned the novel for being Wilde's way of manipulating and corrupting young men with whom he had possible homosexual relationships.

This incidence seems to beg the question: Was Wilde really writing total invention, or was he in fact recording his own life, thoughts, and feelings to an extent? Whether or not Wilde intended to "corrupt" any-body through his writing, the prosecution may have a valid point when they say the novel does reflect occurrences and attitudes that at the time were considered quite dangerous. Wilde wrote perhaps most famously about the three main characters in the novel: "Basil Hallward is what I think I am: Lord Henry what the world thinks of me: Dorian what I would like to be—in other ages perhaps" (*Letters* 352). You might read about Wilde's life in order to discover whether you feel his perceptions about connections between himself and his characters are accurate. What do Basil and Wilde have in common? Why does the world think Wilde is most like Lord Henry? Is that an association that Wilde wants to promote? Why or why not? What evidence in the text shows us this? Why would Wilde have wanted to be like Dorian?

Many novels have prefaces, and many times it is not necessary to read them in order to gain a full understanding of the novel. Not so in *The Picture of Dorian Gray*. Wilde writes a preface that some scholars have argued is actually poetry rather than prose. Reading the preface both before and after reading *The Picture of Dorian Gray* can lend greater insight into the novel:

> *The artist is the creator of beautiful things.*
> *To reveal art and conceal the artist is art's aim.*
> *The critic is he who can translate into another manner or a new*
> 　　*material his impression of beautiful things.*
> *The highest as the lowest form of criticism is a*
> 　　*mode of autobiography.*
> *Those who find ugly meanings in beautiful things are corrupt*
> 　　*without being charming. This is a fault.*
> *Those who find beautiful meanings in beautiful*
> 　　*things are the cultivated. For these there is hope.*
> *They are the elect to whom beautiful things mean only Beauty.*
> *There is no such thing as a moral or an immoral book.*
> *Books are well written, or badly written. That is all.*
> *The nineteenth century dislike of Realism is the rage of Caliban*
> 　　*seeing his own face in a glass.*
> *The nineteenth century dislike of Romanticism is the*
> 　　*rage of Caliban not seeing his own face in a glass.*

The moral life of man forms part of the subject-matter of
    the artist, but the morality of art consists in the perfect use
    of an imperfect medium.
No artist desires to prove anything. Even things that are true can
    be proved.
No artist has ethical sympathies. An ethical sympathy in an
    artist is an unpardonable mannerism of style.
No artist is ever morbid. The artist can express
    everything.
Thought and language are to the artist instruments of an
    art.
Vice and virtue are to the artist materials for an art.
From the point of view of form, the type of all the arts is the art of
    the musician. From the point of view of feeling, the actor's craft is
    the type.
All art is at once surface and symbol.
Those who go beneath the surface do so at their peril.
Those who read the symbol do so at their peril.
It is the spectator, and not life, that art really mirrors.
Diversity of opinion about a work of art shows that the
    work is new, complex, and vital.
When critics disagree an artist is in accord with
    himself.
We can forgive a man for making a useful thing as long as he does
    not admire it. The only excuse for making a useful thing is that one
    admires it immensely.
All art is quite useless. (vii–viii)

Is this poetry? In what ways does it blur the distinction between poetry and prose? Is this preface easier to read as several disconnected ideas, or is it possible to tie them all together? You might choose to look up Wilde's references to Shakespeare (the discussion of Caliban) in order to determine whether or not you agree with Wilde's points. What purpose does it serve for Wilde to even mention Shakespeare in his own preface? Does Shakespeare and/or his work play any sort of role in the rest of the novel?

    Wilde's tone in this preface can be very difficult to gauge. How can we tell when he's being sincere and when he's being facetious or tongue-in-cheek? Look for devices and things like overgeneralizations to try to distinguish between sincerity and insincerity. Sometimes Wilde may be trying to make the opposite point from what he appears to be saying. Which aphorisms in the preface seem to particularly pertain to *The Picture of Dorian Gray*? What does this preface overall reveal about the novel? What does it lead readers to expect? How does it complicate the connection between Wilde and his characters? Do any of the statements in the preface contradict each other? How so? Who are the artists in *Dorian*, according to the definition Wilde gives in the preface? Who are the critics?

However you answer these questions, whichever you decide to pursue, it is clear that Dorian Gray lives today in the original novel and as a general character type (for example, the film *The League of Extraordinary Gentlemen* has a Dorian Gray figure). The preface makes us question, the undertones make us think. The story endures.

TOPICS AND STRATEGIES

This section of the chapter discusses various possible topics for essays on *The Picture of Dorian Gray* and general approaches to these topics. Be aware that the material below is only a place to start from, not some kind of master key to the perfect essay. Use this material to prompt your own thinking. Every topic discussed here could encompass a wide variety of effective papers.

Themes

The Picture of Dorian Gray is a text rich with themes. A theme in a literary work is an idea, an action, an occurrence, or a system that in some way threads itself throughout the book. Themes are often identifiable through a close reading of words, phrases, ideas, and even chapter titles, and they are recognizable as something about which the character(s) and/or author appear to have much to say. In other words, if a book's action and/or characters continually return to a similar idea, you have probably identified a theme of the book. If you decide you would like to write about greed in *The Picture of Dorian Gray*, for example, you might start by asking yourself which character's opinions on or portrayal of greed Wilde seems to be endorsing. Why do you think Wilde does this? What evidence can you find within the text that demonstrates Wilde's support of this character's actions or opinions? How does this influence readers' perceptions of the character, plot, theme, or novel in general?

A theme of a novel and the moral of a novel can overlap in many different ways. Of the moral in his own work, Wilde writes:

> The real moral of the story is that all excess, as well as all renunciation, brings its punishment, and this moral is so far artistically and deliberately suppressed that it does not enunciate its law as a general principle, but realizes itself purely in the lives of individuals, and so becomes simply a dramatic element in a work of art, and not the object of the work of art itself. Is this an artistic error? I fear it is. It is the only error in the book. (*Letters* 263)

What does the novel reveal about excess? Can this also be considered a theme? Why does Wilde claim that the moral of punishment for excess is suppressed? Does he want it that way? Why or why not? Do you interpret the novel in the same way that Wilde does—that the moral is suppressed, coming through individual characters rather than carrying the weight of the entire book?

Sample Topics:

1. **Faustian pact with the devil:** What, overall, is the point that Wilde seems to be making with this theme? Why?

   Selling one's soul to the devil for earthly vanity is surely the most obvious theme in the novel. An interesting question to ask concerning this theme is: Who or what is the devil? Answering "Lord Henry" will lead you down a very different path than answering "society" or "vanity" or "Dorian himself." We know that Dorian sells his soul, but to whom does he sell it? Who or what could cause and/or receive pleasure from seeing the decay in Dorian's morals and conduct? Is *The Picture of Dorian Gray* more concerned with "trying to elicit more from life than life can give" (Ellmann 314)?

2. **Individual nature—greed versus guilt:** Has Dorian been a victim of a system or another person, or does he only have himself to blame?

Who is really in control? The novel "articulates, without offering a clear resolution, the conflict that arises as a result of the struggle within an individual's nature between the impulse toward self-gratification and the sense of guilt that is a consequence of acting upon that inclination" (Gillespie ix). Is it ultimately Dorian who is greedy? Are other characters (Lord Henry, Basil, Sibyl, etc.) greedy in some ways too? Is greed for some things more justifiable or moral than greed for others? At what point do we start to see Dorian feeling guilty about his greediness?

3. **Overlap of art/fiction and life:** Do readers confuse art and life as much as the characters do, perhaps finding the novel eerily similar in some ways to their own lives?

Dorian confuses art with life on purpose, at first hoping that art will bear the brunt of punishment for his lifestyle and eventually realizing the price for such confusion. Wilde wants readers to apply their own thoughts and lives to Dorian's: "Each man sees his own sin in Dorian Gray. What Dorian Gray's sins are no one knows. He who finds them has brought them" (*Letters* 266). Have readers through history generally related to Dorian more than the other characters? Do we attribute our own faults to him? Why? What purpose does it serve for Wilde to use Dorian as a sort of mirror for his readers?

Character

Male characters are more fully realized than female characters in the novel. Sibyl is undeveloped—more like a backdrop against which Dorian's life and personality is revealed. It is the men, and the relationships between them, that hold readers' attention. Does this add a homosexual dimension to the work? The undertone is certainly there, and yet scholars are unable to point to direct references/passages as proof.

You might also ask questions about individual characters, allowing in-depth study. Do we like Dorian? Are we supposed to? Is our sympathy reserved for Basil Hallward? How does Lord Henry manage to instigate so much of the action while remaining almost completely outside of it?

Scholars have claimed that characters in *The Picture of Dorian Gray* have few redeeming qualities, making the novel more of a cautionary tale than a model for emulation. Wilde's response to criticism from the editor of *Lippincott's Monthly* (where *Dorian* was originally published as a novella) addresses this point:

> Bad people are, from the point of view of art, fascinating studies. They represent colour, variety and strangeness. Good people exasperate one's reason; bad people stir one's imagination. Your critic, if I must give him so honourable a title, states that the people in my story have no counterpart in life. . . . Quite so. If they existed they would not be worth writing about. The function of the artist is to invent, not to chronicle. There are no such people. If there were I would not write about them. Life by its realism is always spoiling the subject-matter of art. The supreme pleasure in literature is to realize the non-existent. (*Letters* 259)

How do we define "good" and "bad" when discussing these characters? Why? How does Wilde seem to be defining those terms? Why? How is it that readers seem to relate to Dorian in particular, when Wilde claims that his characters are pure invention rather than reflections of reality?

Sample Topics:

1. **Lord Henry Wotton:** Is he "the miserable end of Dorian himself" (Pater)?

   Is he the devil, or at least the devil's advocate? (Keep the Faustian theme in mind.) If Lord Henry is the devil, is he aware of this role? Does he manipulate Dorian with intention, or does he simply make a few broad comments that Dorian interprets in ways other than Lord Henry intends? It is interesting to note that Lord *Harry* is a common name for the devil and characters refer to Lord Henry as Harry several times in the book.

2. **Dorian:** Is he a victim of Lord Henry? Basil? Society? Is Dorian fully responsible for his actions?

   What implications do Dorian's position as victim or aggressor have on the action/theme of the novel? What, you might ask, is this guy's problem? Does Dorian actually make a conscious pact with the devil, or does he simply articulate a seemingly idle wish that is acted upon by some malicious person or force? Dorian's age and people's perception of his age are key components of the novel. At what points does Dorian seem younger than his actual age? At what points does he seem older than his actual age? He does not age physically, but what are the events and ideas that cause him to age mentally? What bearing does this have on the action and climax of the book? Wilde writes, "Dorian Gray has not got a cool, calculating, conscienceless character at all. On the contrary, he is extremely impulsive, absurdly romantic, and is haunted all through his life by an exaggerated sense of conscience which mars his pleasures for him and warns him that youth and enjoyment are not everything in the world. It is finally to get rid of the conscience that had dogged his steps from year to year that he destroys the picture; and thus in his attempt to kill conscience Dorian Gray kills himself." (*Letters* 263–64)

3. Basil Hallward: What, ultimately, is his role in the novel?

Is he the last person to truly see Dorian before the pact with the devil is made? What can we infer from the fact that Basil worries that Dorian's portrait contains too much of himself (Basil)? Is Basil in love with Dorian? In what ways might the answer to that question affect our interpretations of the novel? Is the portrait, a reflection of Dorian's soul, more beautiful because of Basil's influence on or inclusion in it? Lord Henry says, "Good artists exist simply in what they make, and consequently are perfectly uninteresting in what they are" (41). Is Basil really afraid that *he* is revealed (his soul) in the portrait, or is he afraid that his love for Dorian is revealed?

4. Sibyl Vane: Why does Sibyl kill herself? What does Dorian's reaction to her death reveal about him?

What is it about Sibyl that suddenly disgusts Dorian—is she too real, not artificial enough? How is this both ironic and exactly what readers should have expected from Dorian? Lord Henry consoles Dorian over Sibyl's death by stating that she "was less real" than the fictional roles she played (75). In what way is Sibyl's name appropriate? Ironic? Dorian tells Lord Henry: "Her trust makes me faithful, her belief makes me good. When I am with her, I regret all that you have taught me. I become different from what you have known me to be. I am changed, and the mere touch of Sibyl Vane's hand makes me forget you and all your wrong, fascinating, poisonous, delightful theories" (56). Could Sibyl have saved Dorian? Does he already believe in Lord Henry's theories too much? Does it matter if the spell is already cast?

History and Context

Studying history and context always involves research, and you can begin by choosing a character, a scene, a theme, or a setting from the novel and enquiring as to whether that is what things were really like. Be aware that sometimes the time period in which the action of the work takes place can be different from the time in which the work was written and published, and even the difference of a few years can make a big difference. Once you have determined the similarities and differences between the real world and the Wildean one, you can begin to speculate about what Wilde is trying to convey through his portrayal.

History and context might also pertain to the author's biography. Are there details about Wilde's life or beliefs that add depth and understanding to our reading of this novel?

Whether or not you feel that Victorian society is accurately reflected in *The Picture of Dorian Gray*, there can be no doubt that the novel was presumed to be an accurate reflection of Wilde's ideologies and lifestyle. Any homosexual overtones in the book were used by the marquess of Queensberry's defense attorney, Edward Carson, as evidence that Wilde had corrupted Lord Alfred ("Bosie") Douglas, Queensberry's son. Its use in Wilde's trials make this novel an important text in the social and legal history of literature.

The novel came about because Wilde was invited by the editor of *Lippincott's Monthly,* an American magazine, to contribute an entire story in 1890. Robert Harborough Sherard, Wilde's friend and first biographer, writes:

Oscar Wilde was at that time when the order reached him in consider-able financial embarrassment, and people who saw him then, remember how delighted he was, poor fellow, with an order, which promised him a welcome emolument. It is not conceivable that under these circum-stances he would deliberately write a book of corrupt morals, calculated to pervert. . . . This was one of the charges which were brought against him at the trial. . . . If there be such hideous immorality in the book as certain perceive, Oscar Wilde must have written it unconsciously. (305, 307)

Wilde had not yet met Bosie when he wrote *Dorian,* a fact that effectively eliminates the possibility that he wrote the book with the express pur-pose of corrupting this particular young man. Still, Wilde was sentenced to two years in prison doing hard labor.

Sample Topics:

1. **Faust legend in popular culture:** What are some of the connec-tions and differences between Wilde's novel and other versions of the Faust legend? What is significant about these similarities and differences?

   Faust is a German legend used by writers and musicians such as Christopher Marlowe, Johann Wolfgang von Goethe, Thomas Mann, Hector Berlioz, Franz Liszt, and Washington Irving. Common understanding and interpretation of the legend gen-erally reduces it to a pact between a man and the devil and/ or a man whose vanity and pride lead to his downfall. Wilde would have been familiar with the legend in general and some of these interpretations in particular. In a letter to the editor of the *Scots Observer* in 1890 Wilde writes that "it is a pity that Goethe never had an opportunity of reading *Dorian Gray.* I feel quite certain that he would have been delighted by it" (*Letters* 269).

   Does Wilde's version reveal anything in particular about late Victorian England? If so, what? Why might Wilde have chosen to document or critique society in this way/form?

2. **West End scandal (or the Cleveland Street Affair):** Does this part of *The Picture of Dorian Gray*'s historical context make 19th-century readers' responses dramatically different from 21st-century readers' responses?

Just a few months before Wilde published *The Picture of Dorian Gray,* one member of the English royal family was supposedly involved in "loathsome and disgusting practices" (i.e., homosexuality). The events were sensationalized and eventually involved members of government too. The investigation and fascination went on for five months, ending just 60 days before *Dorian* was first printed. Conduct some research on the West End scandals to determine the effect these events may have had on Wilde's work and the public's perception of it. Does this explain why American readers liked *Dorian* much better (or at least sooner) than English readers?

3. *Dorian's* **role in Wilde's trial:** Is it ironic that Wilde warned against connecting writing too closely with its author's life?

The Real Trial of Oscar Wilde, written by Wilde's grandson, Merlin Holland, can be a real help to you in writing about this topic. What role, specifically, did the novel play in Wilde's trials? Why? Are there other examples in history or current events of a person's art being used against them in a court of law? How is all of this ironic, given the premise in the book that confuses art with life?

Philosophy and Ideas

Philosophy and ideas in a novel are similar to theme, but they are more general, or more universal. Writing about the philosophy and ideas in a book means that you identify broad philosophical ideas and investigate the ways in which the book comments on them. Outside research can be important, but your main focus should be the book (primary text) itself.

In some circles, Wilde's philosophies concerning aestheticism are better known than his actual literary works. It is ironic that Wilde is associated with the "art for art's sake" slogan, which he had rejected even before writing *Dorian*. It is important to remember that Wilde's work (and perhaps his mind) usually operates on at least two levels, and it is often difficult to tell where Wilde's sincere beliefs lie. Wilde biographer Richard Ellmann writes that "For Wilde, aestheticism was not a creed but a problem" (310).

Sample Topics:

1. **Epicureanism:** Which characters seem to have adopted this philosophy? Basil? Sibyl?

   Epicureanism posits that in order to attain the greatest good, one should seek modest pleasures to attain happiness and freedom from fear or physical pain. The philosophy requires knowledge of the world and limits of desire. How does such a philosophy fit into a book in which it seems that no limits are observed?

2. **Hedonism:** Does Wilde seem to support hedonism?

   For hedonists, pleasure is the most important goal, and this book is a tragedy because of this single-minded pursuit of pleasure. In *The Picture of Dorian Gray*, the most blatant hedonist is Lord Henry. Lord Henry gets some of the most memorable lines in the novel. Is he supposed to be a villain because he subscribes to this philosophy? Does Lord Henry adopt the philosophy for himself or merely advocate it for others?

3. **Aestheticism:** Which characters subscribe to aestheticism? Does Wilde seem to be promoting the philosophy or condemning it?

   Aestheticists argue that arts should provide "refined sensuous pleasure, rather than convey moral or sentimental messages." Is it ironic, then, that Wilde was aestheticism's poster boy when *Dorian* certainly contains a moral message? What about Hallward—is he a believer in aestheticism? Hallward contradicts himself in the novel, first worrying that "it is rather the painter who, on the coloured canvas, reveals himself" (4) and then claiming that "Form and colour tell us of form and colour—that is all. It often seems to me that art conceals the artist far more than it ever reveals him" (84). Richard Ellmann posits that *"Dorian Gray* is the aesthetic novel *par excellence,* not in espousing the doctrine, but in exhibiting its dangers," most notably through Dorian's "unintentional suicide, [through which] Dorian becomes aestheticism's first martyr" (315).

Form and Genre

The way in which a book is written and presented can have an enormous impact on readers' reception and interpretations. The form that a work takes involves its shape and structure—chapter length, format, etc. A work's genre is its classification. These elements are often inseparable from content, and so often the purpose of a paper on form and/or genre is to argue for particular interpretations of the content based on the chosen form or genre.

There are several interesting questions to ask about Wilde's overall form and genre in *The Picture of Dorian Gray.* How do you tell a story that is already so widely known? And then how do you reconstruct that story from one form (novella) to another (novel)? Why is this the only extended prose work Wilde ever wrote?

Sample Topics:

1. **Western folklore/myth:** How is it that Wilde can reconstruct a very old story in order to tell a relatively new one that will itself turn into a myth or part of folklore?

   Wilde's purpose is "to retell a story whose end is known" (McCormack 111). Why does he use the basic story fabric rather than completely inventing his own? How is it that *The Picture of Dorian Gray* is one of those stories known even by people who have not read it? What is it in particular about the way in which Wilde tells this story that resonates with readers?

2. **Novella and novel:** In what ways are the two works the same? Why are these similarities important?

The novella of *The Picture of Dorian Gray* was published in *Lippincott's Magazine* in June 1890, edited (and cut) by American editor J. Marshall Stoddart. Americans loved it, English reviewers did not. The novel version, published in 1891, "present[s] some of [Wilde's] more daring ideas in a less direct fashion" (Gillespie xii). Wilde made some changes before the novel was published, such as eliminating much of the homosexual suggestion between Basil and Dorian. It is interesting to note that Stoddart, the magazine editor, made his own changes before publication, and it was this version, rather than his own original, that Wilde revised for the novel. So in some sense there are three existing versions.

3. **Modern morality tale:** What *is* the moral here? Why was Wilde trying to hide it, or at least make it less obvious?

The Picture of Dorian Gray was dubbed a "modern morality tale" by American novella readers. How does this differ from the English response to the novella and novel? Perhaps the greatest irony here is that a novel regarded by some as a morality tale would be used as evidence (literally, in court) for the writer's immorality.

Language, Symbols, and Imagery

To effectively study language, symbols, and imagery you must move beyond unnecessary summary to investigate how the book is written and then make speculations about how these methods of writing and literary elements affect the content of the novel.

Whatever he wanted to portray in terms of content, Wilde was certainly well aware of his choices and skills regarding the novel's style: "So far from wishing to emphasise any moral in my story, the real trouble I experienced in writing the story was that of keeping the extremely obvious moral subordinate to the artistic and dramatic effect" (*Letters* 263). What effects do his choices in this novel have on readers, then and now?

Sample Topics:

1. **Space:** How is space treated in the novel?

Certain activities and conversations take place in certain rooms. How does this add to or detract from the action of the plot? Someone leaves or enters a room at the beginning and end of every chapter. What is the significance of all of this movement? Do particular rooms become symbolic? Is all of this coming and going in itself symbolic?

2. **Murder/knives:** Why is it so often a knife is involved in portrait-related murders?

The portrait is the most obvious symbol in the book, representing Dorian's soul and his external beauty. The destruction of the portrait and the people involved in its creation and power is perhaps the more interesting/subtle symbolism. In chapter two Basil threatens to cut the portrait with his palette-knife: "I will not let it come across our three lives and mar them" (20). Dorian stops him, saying, "It would be murder!" (20). Then in chapter 13, Dorian lets Basil see the altered portrait. Basil says, "I worshipped you too much. I am punished for it. You worshipped yourself too much. We are both punished" (115). Dorian tells him, "It's too late" (115) and stabs him to death. Finally in chapter 20, Dorian finds the knife again: "As it had killed the painter, so it would kill the painter's work, and all that that meant" (164). Dorian's body is later found with a knife through the heart.

3. **Aphorisms/epigrams:** What role does pithy, witty dialogue play in the novel?

Lord Henry has numerous lines of unforgettable dialogue in the novel: "It is only the sacred things that are worth touching" (38), "When one is in love, one always begins by deceiving one's self, and one always ends by deceiving others. That is what the world calls a romance" (38). Why does Lord Henry get all of these concise, witty, memorable lines? This quick wit in conversation is what Wilde was known for. Is this what he meant when he says, "Lord Henry [is] what the world thinks me"?

4. **Dialogue:** What do we learn about characters through what they say and how they say it?

What is the effect of characters revealing themselves through conversation? What do we learn about them through conversation? Why would it have been particularly important for Wilde to make his characters unfold in this way rather than using a lot of authorial intrusion and description?

Compare and Contrast Essays

We can often get a clearer idea of what something is by understanding what it is not, and vice versa. Papers that use comparison and contrast methods include not just lists of similarities and differences but theories and interpretations about why such similarities and differences exist and what effect they have on the novel as a whole.

Dorian does not contain many of the usual character pairings that make comparison and contrast papers for other works a bit easier. Of the relatively few characters in *Dorian*, it is certainly possible to set them next to one another and offer interpretations. Wilde seems more interested, however, in comparing and contrasting more abstract elements in his work, such as Dorian and his portrait, or art and life. He was also intrigued by various art forms, so you will also find comparisons and contrasts between painting and writing in this novel.

Sample Topics:

1. **Basil Hallward and Lord Henry:** What sort of influence does each man have on Dorian?

   Wilde scholar Peter Raby writes that Basil and Lord Henry "in places seem to function as good and evil angel to his Faustus" (69). Is Basil always good, while Lord Henry is always evil? Do Basil's and Lord Henry's roles in the novel eliminate Dorian's responsibility for his own demise?

2. **Wilde and Basil, Henry, or Dorian:** Does Wilde's life play too large a role in readers' responses to *Dorian*?

It is dangerous to conflate a writer's life and personality with his work, perhaps especially in Wilde's case, where nothing is completely straightforward. Yet Wilde himself draws parallels between himself and these three characters. Why? How might such comparison help readers (then and now) understand and evaluate the characters more effectively? Does such inevitable overlap make the concept of "art for art's sake" an unattainable goal?

3. **Dorian and his portrait:** Which is closer to being real?

What does it mean to be "real"? Does Basil in some way create both the portrait and the character/personality of Dorian? While reflecting on his rough treatment of Sybil, Dorian thinks to himself that the picture "held the secret of his life, and told his story. It had taught him to love his own beauty. Would it teach him to loathe his own soul?" (67). After Sibyl's suicide, Dorian tells himself that "The portrait was to bear the burden of his shame: that was all" (77). Does Dorian destroy himself or are others responsible? What literal spaces do Dorian and his portrait occupy? What kinds of things occur when the portrait is present, compared to things that occur when it is hidden or covered? What kind of society is kept by each? Who is allowed (or forbidden) to see the portrait? Who is allowed (or forbidden) to spend time with Dorian? What is Dorian's relationship with his soul (the portrait)? At one point Dorian looks at the portrait and notes that "The very sharpness of the contrast used to quicken his sense of pleasure. He grew more and more enamoured of his own beauty, more and more interested in the corruption of his own soul" (93).

4. **Art and life:** Does the novel focus more on one than the other?

Does Wilde manage (as was his aim) to walk the difficult and tense line between life and art, exploring both? Chapter five (added to 1891 edition) stands out as particularly gritty, leaving Dorian out almost entirely and focusing on Sibyl and her family. In what ways do Sibyl and her family embody the juxtaposition of art and life? Why would Wilde add a chapter like this, which does not really fit into the "prettiness" of the rest of the novel? How does the chapter blend art and life? Near the end of the novel, Lord Henry says to Dorian, "I am so glad that you have never done anything, never carved a statue, or painted a picture, or produced anything outside of yourself! Life has been your art" (160). Dorian's response is, "You don't know everything about me" (160). Is Lord Henry's equation of art and life in Dorian's life part of what drives Dorian to his final act? Why or why not?

Bibliography for *The Picture of Dorian Gray*

Ellmann, Richard. *Oscar Wilde.* New York: Vintage Books, 1988.

Gillespie, Michael Patrick. Preface. *The Picture of Dorian Gray: Authoritative Text, Backgrounds and Contexts, Criticism.* 2d ed. A Norton Critical Edition. New York: W. W. Norton, 2007. ix–xiii.

McCormack, Jerusha. "Wilde's Fiction(s)." *Cambridge Companion to Oscar Wilde.* Ed. Peter Raby. Cambridge: Cambridge UP, 1997. 96–117.

Pater, Walter. "A Novel by Mr. Oscar Wilde." *The Bookman* (November 1891).

Raby, Peter. *Oscar Wilde.* Cambridge: Cambridge UP, 1988.

Sherard, Robert Harborough. *The Life of Oscar Wilde.* London: T. Werner Laurie, 1906.

Wilde, Oscar. *The Letters of Oscar Wilde.* Ed. Rupert Hart-Davis. New York: Harcourt, Brace and World, 1962.

———. *The Picture of Dorian Gray.* 1891. New York: Dover, 1993.

THE IMPORTANCE OF BEING EARNEST

READING TO WRITE

THE IMPORTANCE OF BEING EARNEST is Oscar Wilde's best-known and most popular play. It is imperative to remember the comedic intentions of the play, perhaps best indicated by the subtitle of the work: *A Trivial Comedy for Serious People.* In an interview with Robert Ross, published about a month before the play opened, Wilde said that *The Importance of Being Earnest*'s philosophy was "That we should treat all the trivial things of life seriously and all the serious things of life with sincere and studied triviality" (Pearson xiv).

Scholars take particular note of the ludicrous elements of *The Importance of Being Earnest:* "The play's artificiality and its exaggeration of style and structure, joined to its psychological improbabilities, produce a ludic, fantasy world in which undefined personality may be mutable and, therefore, freely creative" (Jackson 23). Who in the play is "freely creative"? Or is it only Wilde who can be described in that way?

Though it is vital to understand the play as a comedy, it would be a mistake to write it off entirely as a bit of fluff, intended only to entertain rather than criticize or inform. Consider the following passage:

LADY BRACKNELL [*Sternly.*] . . . What are your politics?

JACK. Well, I am afraid I really have none. I am a Liberal Unionist.

LADY BRACKNELL. Oh, they count as Tories. They dine with us. Or come in the evening, at any rate. Now to minor matters. Are your parents living?

JACK. I have lost both my parents.

LADY BRACKNELL. Both? To lose one parent may be regarded as a misfortune—to lose *both* seems like carelessness. Who was your father? He was evidently a man of some wealth. Was he born in what the Radical papers call the purple of commerce, or did he rise from the ranks of the aristocracy?

JACK. I am afraid I really don't know. The fact is, Lady Bracknell, I said I had lost my parents. It would be nearer the truth to say that my parents seem to have lost me. . . . I don't actually know who I am by birth. I was . . . well, I was found.

LADY BRACKNELL. Found!

JACK. The late Mr. Thomas Cardew, an old gentlemen of a very charitable and kindly disposition, found me, and gave me the name of Worthing, because he happened to have a first-class ticket for Worthing in his pocket at the time. Worthing is a place in Sussex. It is a seaside resort.

LADY BRACKNELL. Where did the charitable gentleman who had a first-class ticket for this seaside resort find you?

JACK [*Gravely.*] In a hand-bag.

LADY BRACKNELL. A hand-bag?

JACK [*Very seriously.*] Yes, Lady Bracknell. I was in a hand-bag—a somewhat large, black leather hand-bag, with handles to it—an ordinary hand-bag in fact.

LADY BRACKNELL. In what locality did this Mr James, or Thomas, Cardew come across this ordinary hand-bag?

JACK. In the cloak-room at Victoria Station. It was given to him in mistake for his own.

LADY BRACKNELL. The cloak-room at Victoria Station?

JACK. Yes. The Brighton line.

LADY BRACKNELL. The line is immaterial. Mr Worthing, I confess I feel somewhat bewildered by what you have just told me. To be born, or at any rate bred, in a hand-bag, whether it had handles or not, seems to me to display a contempt for the ordinary decencies of family life that reminds one of the worst excesses of the French Revolution. And I presume you know what that unfortunate movement led to? As for the particular locality in which the hand-bag was found, a cloak-room at a railway station might serve to conceal a social indiscretion—has probably, indeed, been used for that purpose before now—but it could hardly be regarded as an assured basis for a recognized position in good society.

JACK. May I ask you then what you would advise me to do? I need hardly say I would do anything in the world to ensure Gwendolen's happiness.

LADY BRACKNELL. I would strongly advise you, Mr Worthing, to try and acquire some relations as soon as possible, and to make a definite effort to produce at any rate one parent, of either sex, before the season is quite over.

JACK. Well, I don't see how I would possibly manage to do that. I can produce the hand-bag at any moment. It is in my dressing-room at home. I really think that should satisfy you, Lady Bracknell.

LADY BRACKNELL. Me, sir! What has it to do with me? You can hardly imagine that I and Lord Bracknell would dream of allowing our only daughter—a girl brought up with the utmost care—to marry into a

cloak-room, and form an alliance with a parcel? Good morning, Mr
Worthing! (494–95)

Lady Bracknell is clearly dismayed over Jack's lack of prestige and place
in society. To what extent are we to take Lady Bracknell's remarks and
attitude seriously? In other words, to what extent does she represent
actual, serious Victorian ideals and norms? Consider Wilde's very particular point of view:

> [His] stance as a dandy, a performer and (as an Irishman) an outsider
> gave him a particular use for the machinery and conventions both of
> the social world and of the society drama of the theatre, which gave fic-
> tional expression to its values by dwelling on stories of fallen and falling
> women, reinforcing social and sexual discriminations, showing the righ-
> teous but hard consequences of maintaining ideals, and endorsing the
> cruel and absolute exclusion of those who erred. (Jackson 169)

Is Wilde simply making fun of Lady Bracknell and other characters for
taking all of this so seriously, or is there a larger point here?

Think about the historical context of the play as well. What level of
importance would trains and train stations have had in 19th-century
England? Might the train or the station symbolize something here?
Why is Lady Bracknell so afraid of another French Revolution? Does she
reflect popular attitudes and ideas of the time? Does Wilde appear to
share those views? How can you tell?

Lady Bracknell delivers one of Wilde's most famous lines in this
passage: "To lose one parent may be regarded as a misfortune—to lose
both seems like carelessness" (494). If you study the revisions and evolution of the play, this line takes on particular importance. Why did
Wilde revise it the way that he did? What effect might the original line
have had? It can be very useful to look up this information, especially
concerning this line and the deleted fourth act known as the Gribsby
Episode.

The opening night of *The Importance of Being Earnest* was a triumph.
Wilde's friend Ada Leverson "remembered that [on opening night] Wilde
was wearing a coat with a black velvet collar, with white gloves, a green
scarab ring, a large bunch of seals on a black moiré ribbon watch chain
hanging from his white waistcoat; his face was a clear red-brown, and a

green carnation bloomed savagely in his button-hole" (Raby 40). Wilde was at the top of his game, and the play itself was a smash: "According to Allan Aynesworth, who played Algernon Moncrieff, 'In my fifty-three years of acting, I never remember a greater triumph than the first night of *The Importance of Being Earnest*'" (Raby 40).

TOPICS AND STRATEGIES

This section of the chapter addresses various possible topics for writing about *The Importance of Being Earnest* as well as general methods for approaching these topics. These lists are in no way exhaustive and are meant to provide a jumping-off point rather than an answer key. Use these suggestions to find your own ideas and form your own analyses. All topics discussed in this chapter could turn into very effective papers.

Themes

The Importance of Being Earnest is a fun, almost whimsical play that audiences enjoy at many levels. It is easy to get lost in the clever language and upside-down intentions (of both Wilde and the characters) and forget that there are several themes at work here too. A theme is the writer's thoughts and opinions on some of the subjects of the work. It is not just what the work is about—the theme is what the writer/work has to say about the work's subject(s). A theme usually overlays the work and can therefore be found throughout, so look for points when the work returns to particular ideas/subjects. Themes can be revealed through a particular character, in which case you might ask why, for example, does the idea of sacrifice seem to come more often from female characters? What does Wilde seem to be telling us about his views of sacrifice and/or of gender? A theme might also come through in the tone or mood of the work or in its repetition of particular words, concepts, or opinions. Writing about a work's theme requires you to dig below the surface, think about all that the work entails and all that the writer could logically be trying to say, and ask questions like why and how.

Sample Topics:

1. **Matriarchy:** Is matriarchy oppressive or liberating in the play? Does it depend on the character's perspective and/or gender?

Lady Bracknell is clearly in control—but so are Cecily and Gwendolen, to some extent. Jack and Algy have to give up their male-bonding (Bunburying) in order to be considered acceptable by the women. To what extent is the world of the play dominated by women? Is this part of Wilde's inversion—to give women in the play power they would never have in reality—or is it a projection or exaggeration of late Victorian society, centered on women?

2. **Double lives:** Is there anyone in the play who does not live some sort of double life?

How can we tell when we are learning or seeing/hearing the truth from characters who lie and invent so consistently? Does Wilde seem to portray double lives as a necessary evil, harmless fun, or as a simple part of life? Are characters only happy when they are their fictional selves?

3. **Sacrifice:** Which characters in the play choose to make sacrifices? Why? Which characters are forced to make sacrifices? Why?

Do sacrifices stem from selfish motivations, or are characters trying to benefit others as well? You would do well to look at the sacrifice theme on a character-by-character basis rather than trying to lump them all together. What messages about sacrifice does Wilde seem to want the audience to understand? Why? How can we tell? Which characters perceive their actions as sacrifices, and which ones actually make sacrifices?

4. **Values:** How does Wilde's emphasis on the trivial and shallow help readers/audiences to understand that he is actually promoting stronger, more worthy values?

Characters in *The Importance of Being Earnest* are serious about all of the wrong things. For example, while Algernon and Jack are flippant about deceiving everyone they know by creating

alter egos for themselves, Algy says: "I hate people who are not
serious about meals. It is so shallow of them" (487). We begin to
understand that Wilde's point, and the values he seeks to highlight and promote, are precisely the opposite of those espoused
by his characters. What are some of the values that Wilde wants
to promote? How can you tell? Are his methods successful?

Character

It is difficult to dislike any characters in *The Importance of Being Earnest*,
especially when the plot comes full circle at the end. Which character(s)
do you think Wilde intended audiences to like or relate to the most?
Why? How can you tell? Wilde scholar Peter Raby writes that "More
emphatically than in most comedy, these characters are overtly fictional,
dramatic constructs who belong far more to the traditions and conventions of drama than they do to their counterparts in 'real life'" (58).

Do Wilde's characters do more than just decorate the stage and
express ridiculous ideas? Ask yourself after reading the play if you agree
with the following statement: "Wilde's characters both embody and mock
dramatic stereotypes: his formidable dowager, sweet *ingénue*, fussy cler-
gyman and scapegrace man about town lead double lives as parodies of
themselves. . . . His characters are ruthless in the pursuit of selfish goals
and absurd ideals, not combative in the furtherance of the Life-force or
social justice" (Jackson 172). Are the characters helping Wilde to make a
larger point about society, "life-force or social justice"?

Sample Topics:

1. **Lady Bracknell:** To what extent does she represent Victorian
   ideals?

   Does she grow and change in the course of the play? If so, how
   and why? If not, why not? In many ways she is the obstacle
   that the other characters must overcome: Jack must prove to
   her that he is wealthy and stable enough to marry Gwendolen,
   Algernon must find a wife that Lady Bracknell finds suitable
   (and wealthy), Gwendolen must obey her (or at least appear
   to obey her), Cecily must prove herself worthy of Algernon,
   and Miss Prism must finally answer to her regarding the long-

lost baby. Do we ever see a softer side of Lady Bracknell? Does she provide comic relief in the play, or is she a rather stern reminder of the "real" society? Which aspect(s) of society might Lady Bracknell's authority represent?

2. **Algernon Moncrieff:** What has he really been doing while he's Bunburying?

It seems that even by the end of the play we have more questions than answers about Algernon. Some scholars have argued that his Bunburying activities are sexual or even homosexual in nature. Is there evidence of this in the play? If so, how does this change our characterization of Algernon? His appearance at the Worthing country home is not a surprise when we understand Algy's curiosity and desire to foil Jack's plans. But what sort of change comes over Algernon when he meets Cecily? Is he sincerely in love with her or is this some sort of game for him? Will Cecily and Algernon have a happy marriage? Why or why not? How can you tell?

3. **Miss Prism:** What is her actual role in the play's plot?

In some ways, she is the height of shallowness, making the ridiculous mistake of exchanging a baby and a three-volume novel. Still, it seems that no one holds this colossal error against her—part of Wilde's inversion of the serious and the trivial, certainly. How does Miss Prism's union with Chausable illustrate the emphasis on all characters being paired up in the end? How does Miss Prism's life and involvement in Cecily's education both meet and defy gender expectations of Wilde's time?

History and Context

The Importance of Being Earnest has a fascinating history and context, both in terms of the circumstances of its presentation on stage and in terms of the history of societal issues embedded in the play itself. Studying history and context allows us to look beyond the play itself and delve into the ideologies surrounding its creation. Knowing something about Wilde's world and the knowledge and attitudes of his first readers/audiences can add greatly to our interpretation and appreciation of the play.

Sample Topics:

1. **Bunburying as code for Wilde's lifestyle:** Are there clues in the play that suggest homosexuality?

   Alan Sinfield, in *The Wilde Century: Effeminacy, Oscar Wilde, and the Queer Moment,* argues against the interpretation of Bunburying as code for a gay lifestyle, stating that such a reading is anachronistic. Research on Wilde's biography as well as late Victorian society will help you draw your own conclusions about the extent to which Wilde's lifestyle is reflected in the play. Be aware of Wilde's tendency toward sarcasm, satire, and inversion. These tactics tend to keep readers at a distance, making definitive conclusions extremely difficult to make (though that very quality also indicates that this topic is a good one).

2. **Queensberry:** How did Queensberry's role in Wilde's life influence the play and its reception?

   When *The Importance of Being Earnest* opened at St. James's Theatre on February 14, 1895, the marquess of Queensberry was there, prepared to make an ugly scene. Wilde had heard of these plans and instructed the business manager to return money Queensberry had sent to ensure himself a ticket. Queensberry ended up leaving only "a grotesque bouquet of vegetables for Wilde at the stage door" (Raby 40). Queensberry was the father of Lord Alfred Douglas ("Bosie"), with whom Wilde had been in a relationship.

3. **New Woman:** To what extent do Cecily, Gwendolen, Miss Prism, and/or Lady Bracknell embody the characteristics of the New Woman?

   This play includes and even emphasizes women to a large degree. Perhaps in some ways the characters themselves seem like throwbacks to an earlier time, especially with their obsessions over marriage. But if you consider Wilde's inversion technique enough to realize that he is often making the opposite point of what is emphasized in the play, our reading changes dramatically. Do the women themselves seem to understand their own ridiculousness on some level? Do they seem like the kinds of women who will sit back and let their husbands control the household? In what ways do the female characters fit into the Victorian idea of womanhood? In what ways do they fit into an early 20th-century view of womanhood? Is Wilde trying to be contradictory and confusing or does he have a different point to make?

4. **Victorian sensibilities:** If *The Importance of Being Earnest* is a satire, or parody, of Victorian lifestyle and ordeals, which aspects does Wilde seem to be attacking?

Lady Bracknell seems, in some ways, to be holding up the old-fashioned end of things. She says, for example: "An engagement should come on a young girl as a surprise, pleasant or unpleasant, as the case may be. It is hardly a matter that she could be allowed to arrange for herself" (492). Audiences understand that this idea is supposed to appear ludicrous, and they did even in Wilde's time. Yet for many, lines like these might also reflect their own lifestyle, values, and ideals. Does Wilde pose any solutions for the problems he takes on in the play? What is his purpose for writing about his own time in this way? Peter Raby writes that "The play functions through the meticulous imitation, and then subversion, of the tribal social customs of upper-class late Victorian society" (41).

Philosophy and Ideas

It is easy to do a surface-level reading of *The Importance of Being Earnest*, and yet if you are reading carefully it becomes difficult to miss Wilde's philosophy and ideas embedded within. Philosophy and ideas in a literary work are similar to theme in some ways, but they address the wider world through commentary on large, sometimes even universal, ideas. Wilde was in some circles better known for his philosophy than for his writing, so it is important to study this aspect of *The Importance of Being Earnest.*

Sample Topics:

1. **Hedonism:** Does the end of Jack and Algy's Bunburying contradict their otherwise hedonistic lifestyle, or does it somehow serve their interests as well?

   Hedonism involves an existence that is (or strives to be) entirely for pleasure. Jack and Algy both live (and will continue to live) lives of idleness, searching for happiness and unconcerned with other people or issues. The first conversation that we see between Algy and Jack (who is pretending to be Ernest) begins with this idea: "ALGERNON. What brings you up to town? JACK. Oh, pleasure, pleasure! What else should bring one anywhere?" (481).

2. **Dandy versus gentleman:** How does the play define masculinity? How does it display masculinity?

   In Victorian England, manliness included (among other things) "honesty, vigor, asceticism, virility, loyalty, industry, piety, candidness and earnestness" (Foldy 83). Dandies, on the other hand, paid particular attention to their appearance, lived leisurely lives, and spoke in refined (if not eloquent) language. Why does there not seem to be any middle ground between the two extremes? It appears that a man would have to make fairly deliberate choices in order to be clearly seen as either a dandy or a gentleman. What might drive or inspire some of those choices? In what ways was choosing a particular type of masculinity a way of displaying one's philosophies of life, society, love, and lifestyle? Jack and Algy are both very much dandies. Are there any gentlemen in the play? If not, why? How does Wilde seem to be defining masculinity in the play?

3. **Marriage:** What philosophies of marriage does Wilde seem to convey in *The Importance of Being Earnest*?

Which characters promote these philosophies, and how does that affect our interpretation of the ideas? Do the characters ever agree on the topic of marriage? Why or why not? How can you tell when Wilde is being serious about marriage and when he is using humor or inverting his true philosophy? Algernon is certainly negative about marriage in the beginning: "It is very romantic to be in love. But there is nothing romantic about a definite proposal. Why, one may be accepted. One usually is, I believe. Then the excitement is all over" (482). How do the female characters' views on marriage differ from the male characters' views? Is Wilde using their opinions on marriage to make fun of one or both of the genders? Does the play's ending provide an optimistic view of marriage? Why or why not? How can you tell?

Form and Genre

Form and genre provide ways of classifying works that usually allow us to study them more fully. Form is defined as the style and structure of a work, whereas genre is the type, or classification, of a work. Both form and genre are usually distinct from a work's content, though writers use each of them quite specifically in order to convey a particular message, reach a certain audience, or to simply strengthen the impact of their work.

Of *The Importance of Being Earnest,* several scholars agree that "Although described by some critics as a farcical comedy, it is so much superior in wit to any work of the kind in the language, that the description is meaningless. It comes under no category. It is unique, like its author" (Pearson xvi).

Sample Topics:

1. **Three acts:** What does the Gribsby episode add to or take away from the play as we know it?

   The Importance of Being Earnest was originally a four-act play, but George Alexander convinced Wilde to cut one of the acts. Wilde protested: "The scene which you feel is superfluous cost me terrible exhausting labor and heart-rending nerve-racking strain. You may not believe me, but I assure you on my honor that it must have taken fully five minutes to write" (Pearson xiv). In the deleted act, a character named Mr. Gribsby is trying to arrest Algernon (who he thinks is Ernest Worthing) for debts that Jack incurred while "Bunburying." If placed back into the play, this "Gribsby Episode" would occur in Act Two, just after Jack has discovered Algy ("Ernest") at the country house.

2. **Wit:** What exactly makes this play witty, as opposed to simply funny?

The 19th century had seen and read plenty of comedy, like Charles Dickens's popular book, *The Posthumous Papers of the Pickwick Club.* But people had rarely encountered wit like Oscar Wilde's: "JACK. I wish to goodness we had a few fools left. ALGERNON. We have. JACK. I should extremely like to meet them. What do they talk about? ALGERNON. The fools? Oh! about the clever people, of course. JACK. What fools!" (496). Critic William Archer wrote of *The Importance of Being Earnest* as "An absolutely willful expression of an irrepressibly witty personality" (quoted in Pearson xv). Wit has a certain sophistication, or complicatedness, to it that seems to take it to a higher level than comedy.

3. **Stage direction:** Do the stage directions make the play easier to read? What would the play be like without them?

Playwrights use stage direction in many ways. Shakespeare's works have little or no stage direction, for example, while *The Importance of Being Earnest* has stage direction that is quite specific: "*Gwendolen goes to the door. She and Jack blow kisses to each other behind Lady Bracknell's back. Lady Bracknell looks vaguely about as if she could not understand what the noise was. Finally turns round*" (492). Does this specific information make the parts easier for actors, or more difficult? Do film versions of *The Importance of Being Earnest* follow Wilde's direction? Why or why not? What impact does this have on the film and its ability to bring Wilde's intention to the screen? If there is too much stage direction, does it indicate that the piece should have been in another form or genre—short story, etc.?

4. **Psychological farce:** Is it really more complicated than it first appears to be?

Certainly *The Importance of Being Earnest* is a social comedy, indicting many Victorian ideals and ways of life. Even readers and audiences today can recognize shallow aspects of their society in the play. But in what way is the play a psychological farce?

Language, Symbols, and Imagery

There are a lot of particularities in *The Importance of Being Earnest* that add up to the play's rather unique tone. Wilde's choices regarding topics and themes could convey a certain cynicism, but instead he uses language, symbols, and imagery to create a much more lighthearted atmosphere or mood, even considering the fact that many readers and audience members will mull over the themes and topics long after the play is finished.

Many readers, scholars, and audience members credit Wilde with giving them a new appreciation for language and the ways in which it can be used for particular effect. Wilde uses imagery in *The Importance of Being Earnest,* creating a rather idyllic country world as a backdrop for most of the play's action, and surely there is plenty of symbolism in things like the train station and the handbag. But it is the language that is Wilde's true masterpiece here.

Some scholars argue that language is the pivotal point in this play—more important, even, than the characters.

Sample Topics:

1. **Inversion:** If what seems to be important is actually trivial, and vice versa, how can we tell what Wilde is really trying to emphasize?

Inversion occurs not only in terms of characters but at the sentence and word level too. The most obvious example is the name Ernest. Algernon brings up the name's connotation right away: "You look as if your name was Ernest. You are the most earnest looking person I ever saw in my life" (484). As the play progresses we see that the true importance of being earnest is, as far as the characters are concerned, wrapped up entirely in the name Ernest, while in fact it is not at all important to possess or demonstrate the trait of earnestness. This inversion helps Wilde to make the opposite point from his characters. Audiences see how petty and ridiculous the characters are, and therefore see that it is earnestness, rather than the name Ernest, that is truly important.

2. **Aphorisms:** Does one character speak in aphorisms more than another? Why might this be?

Wilde's writing can be very pithy, almost making one wish that he were with us today, since he would surely be a master of the witty soundbite. Pick out some of the most striking, mind-bending aphorisms and examine them carefully. Do there seem to be themes or philosophies running through the aphorisms? Why might Wilde choose to highlight these themes or philosophies in this manner? Consider the following two sentences, and think about what they may have in common: "More than half of modern culture depends on what one shouldn't read" (483). "The truth is rarely pure and never simple. Modern life would be very tedious if it were either, and modern literature a complete impossibility!" (485).

3. **Figurative language:** Does Wilde use figurative language with all characters or only with particular individuals? Why?

Part of the joy of reading *The Importance of Being Earnest* resides in finding the multiple meanings behind several of Wilde's words. Gwendolen, for example, explains to Cecily that "Mamma, whose views on education are remarkably strict, has brought me up to be extremely short-sighted; it is part of her system; so do you mind my looking at you through my glasses?" (516). Of course we understand the meaning of "short-sighted" to be both literal, explaining Gwendolen's need for glasses, and figurative, in the sense that Gwendolen is incapable of seeing long-term or far-reaching consequences. The fact that Lady Bracknell has fostered this inability adds another layer of humor. What does such language do to affect our reading? Does it serve to make readers/audiences feel smarter than characters like Gwendolen and Cecily? How so? How does this influence our characterizations?

Compare and Contrast Essays

Characters, places, and actions in *The Importance of Being Earnest* can often seem so in sync that it is difficult to pull them apart for the purposes of comparing or contrasting them. Yet doing so can force us to read more carefully and understand the work more fully.

Comparisons and contrasts cannot just be made for their own sake. They have to have a point or, in other words, a larger purpose. Anytime you start comparing or contrasting characters, places, events, or ideas, carefully consider what effect this has on the work as a whole, on audience reception, on theme or philosophy, on authorial intent, etc.

Sample Topics:

1. **City and country:** How does Wilde characterize each location? Are people more gullible, more boring in one place than in another?

Are Algy and Jack able to get away with deceptions in one location that they would not possibly pull off in another location? Do events in the play support Jack's observation, that "When one is in town one amuses oneself. When one is in the country one amuses other people" (481)? Lady Bracknell says: "A girl with a simple, unspoiled nature, like Gwendolen, could hardly be expected to reside in the country" (493). Wilde seems to be inverting literary scheme too, as readers/audiences would normally expect young people to be corrupted by the city rather than the country, as Lady Bracknell implies. Gwendolen is presumably the sophisticated city lady, while Cecily is the natural country girl. Does Wilde stick with these stereotypical characterizations, or does he refute them?

2. **Gwendolen and Cecily:** Are these young women more similar than they are different?

In what ways does each woman defy stereotypes and expectations of women in their time? How do the two women together reveal Wilde's attitudes toward women? Fairly early on, Gwendolen and Cecily are enemies, competing for "Ernest." Just as quickly, they declare themselves best friends. Are either of these relationships sincere? Both women like to imagine themselves as sophisticated individuals. Is this accurate? Is one woman more sophisticated than the other? What point does Wilde seem to be making about their levels of sophistication?

3. **Jack Worthing and Ernest Montcrieff:** Do we get any sense that Jack's personality will change now that he is actually named Ernest?

Of course we assume his lifestyle will change, since he will be married, but will the man himself actually become different in any fundamental way(s)?

Bibliography for *The Importance of Being Earnest*

Foldy, Michael S. *The Trials of Oscar Wilde: Deviance, Morality, and the Late Victorian Society.* New Haven: Yale UP, 1997.

Jackson, Russell. "*The Importance of Being Earnest.*" *Cambridge Companion to Oscar Wilde.* Ed. Peter Raby. Cambridge: Cambridge UP, 1997. 161–77.

Nunokawa, Jeff, and Amy Sickels. *Oscar Wilde.* Gay & Lesbian Writers Series. Lesléa Newman, series editor. Philadelphia: Chelsea House, 2005.

Pearson, Hesketh. Introduction. *Five Plays.* By Oscar Wilde. New York: Bantam Books, 1961. vii–xvi.

Raby, Peter. *The Importance of Being Earnest: A Reader's Companion.* Twayne's Masterwork Series no. 144. New York: Twayne, 1994.

Siebold, Thomas, ed. *Readings on The Importance of Being Earnest*. Greenhaven Press Literary Companion Series. San Diego: Greenhaven Press, 2001.

Wilde, Oscar. *The Importance of Being Earnest: A Trivial Comedy for Serious People*. 1895. *Oscar Wilde: The Major Works*. Ed. Isobel Murray. Oxford: Oxford UP, 2000. 477–538.

THE HAPPY PRINCE

READING TO WRITE

OSCAR WILDE wrote in many forms and genres, but perhaps the most interesting and surprisingly complicated are his fairy tales. Scholars often wonder why Wilde wrote fairy tales at all: "Far from being the cause of frivolity and his Aesthetic Camp, Wilde's homosexuality led to a deepening of the human capability for love and the willingness to sacrifice all for a beloved. The only literary form in which he could record this change of heart was the fairy tale. Wilde's legacy to his sons was the journal of his own heart" (Martin 77).

Certainly we know that Wilde read to and wrote fairy tales for his two sons, Cyril and Vyvyan. Perhaps he was also influenced by his wife, Constance Wilde, who published two children's books, *There was once: Grandma's Stories* and *A Long Time Ago*, in the same year Wilde published *The Happy Prince & Other Tales* (Shillinglaw 82). Regardless of his reasons for writing in this genre, Wilde certainly provides readers with plenty to think about after reading tales like *The Happy Prince.*

It is important to read works like this closely rather than disregarding them for being just children's stories. The following passage from *The Happy Prince* is filled with potential paper topics:

At that moment a curious crack sounded inside the statue, as if something had broken. The fact is that the leaden heart had snapped right in two. It certainly was a dreadfully hard frost.

Early the next morning the Mayor was walking in the square below in company with the Town Councillors. As they passed the column he looked up at the statue: 'Dear me! how shabby the Happy Prince looks!' he said.

'How shabby indeed!' cried the Town Councillors, who always agreed with the Mayor, and they went up to look at it.

'The ruby has fallen out of his sword, his eyes are gone, and he is golden no longer,' said the Mayor; in fact, he is little better than a beggar!'

'Little better than a beggar,' said the Town Councillors.

'And here is actually a dead bird at his feet!' continued the Mayor. 'We must really issue a proclamation that birds are not to be allowed to die here.' And the Town Clerk made a note of the suggestion.

So they pulled down the statue of the Happy Prince. 'As he is no longer beautiful he is no longer useful,' said the Art Professor at the University.

Then they melted the statue in a furnace, and the Mayor held a meeting of the Corporation to decide what was to be done with the metal. 'We must have another statue, of course,' he said, 'and it shall be a statue of myself.'

'Of myself,' said each of the Town Councillors, and they quarreled. When I last heard of them they were quarrelling still.

'What a strange thing!' said the overseer of the workmen at the foundry. 'This broken lead heart will not melt in the furnace. We must throw it away.' So they threw it on a dustheap where the dead Swallow was also lying.

'Bring me the two most precious things in the city,' said God to one of His Angels; and the Angel brought Him the leaden heart and the dead bird.

'You have rightly chosen,' said God, 'for in my garden of Paradise this little bird shall sing for evermore, and in my city of gold the Happy Prince shall praise me.'

Consider Wilde's use of language in this passage. We can see that "the leaden heart had snapped right in two" both literally and metaphorically, in this case (34). In what other ways does Wilde use figurative language? Does such language indicate that he is writing for children, or does it require the sophistication of adult readers? Does the story demonstrate Wilde's "rather patronizing views concerning the tastes and reasoning of children as mere miniature adults" (Roditi 71)?

You might also think about the larger context of the tale. What can we learn about Wilde's own relationship with God (or lack thereof) from this tale? Are the religious overtones here straightforward? Are they particular to one religion? How can you tell? Is there anything ironic or particularly stylized about religion in this tale? You might take a biographical approach to the tale in this case, studying Wilde's personal life and religious beliefs next to *The Happy Prince* in order to gain insight.

TOPICS AND STRATEGIES

This section of the chapter addresses various possible topics for writing about *The Happy Prince* as well as general methods for approaching these topics. These lists are in no way exhaustive and are meant to provide a jumping-off point rather than an answer key. Use these suggestions to find your own ideas and form your own analyses. All topics discussed in this chapter could yield very effective papers.

Themes

How is a theme different from the moral of a story? Fairy tales are expected to share some sort of message, or moral, with readers (who are usually children). Do any of Wilde's messages fulfill criteria for both a theme and a moral? How does this help us understand who Wilde's intended audience may have been?

To effectively study and write about a work's theme, look for words, phrases, and ideas that are somehow emphasized—through repetition, for example. Remember that a theme is different from a subject. The subject is what the work is about, while the theme is what the work or author has to say about the subject.

Sample Topics:

1. **Charity:** Is there more than simple charity behind the prince's and the swallow's actions?

   Charity can become a negative thing, if those who work with or donate to charity see themselves as higher, better, more moral, or more worthy than those accepting the charity. What is Wilde's message about charity in *The Happy Prince*? How

can you tell? What is the difference between donating posses-
sions and giving a part of oneself? Which of these do the swallow and the happy prince accomplish? How can you tell?

2. **Self-denial:** In what ways are self-denial and mercy the same
thing? Is it possible to have one without the other?

How do the prince and the swallow deny themselves things?
How does their self-denial become a form of mercy toward
others? Is the prince's self-denial too little, too late? Would
poor townspeople have been better served if he had been more
merciful during his life? What is the fairy tale's message about
self-denial? Is this message the same for both adults and children? Why or why not?

3. **The power of the spoken wish:** Why does it seem like people
are often afraid to speak their wishes out loud?

Wilde employs this theme in other works as well—*The Picture of Dorian Gray*, for instance. How does *The Happy Prince*
teach readers to not only speak their own wishes but work to
make the wishes of others come true? How does Wilde's message about the power of the spoken wish change or remain the
same in his various works conveying this theme?

4. **Renunciation:** Does Wilde appear to be rejecting or embracing
elements of his own life in this tale?

The prince renounces his life in the palace, and the swallow
in some ways renounces his flight to Spain: "This element of
renunciation in the tale, combined with its composition in the
years immediately following Wilde's marriage (in 1884) and
the birth of his sons, has led many critics to see this tale and
others as statements of an attempt to reject homosexuality"
(Martin 75). At the same time, other critics see the relationship between the prince and the swallow as Wilde's attempt to
embrace homosexuality.

Character

Characters can be written about in several different ways, including: character development, methods of characterization, and even how we determine who is a character and who is not. When you write about character, you need to determine how we as readers get to know the characters in the story. The ways in which an author leaks information about a character can be as important as the characterization itself. Do we learn the most about the Happy Prince through his own words? Through his actions? Through the other characters' reactions to him, or conversations about him? How does the swallow serve as a window into the Happy Prince's characterization? How does Wilde differentiate his characters, and how does he make them seem so real to us (or doesn't he)? It is important to look at character in terms of broad strokes like which specific actions certain characters take, but it is equally important to study the methods of characterization that are easy to overlook: a character's manner of speaking, the images or setting connected with a character, repetition of words and phrases associated with a character, other characters' reactions to and discussions about a character, and the narrator's (and/or author's) commentary about a character.

Who is the true hero of this story? Fairy tales generally have very few characters, and sometimes this might mean that one character embodies or represents actions and points of view of several people or types of people. Is this true of characters in *The Happy Prince*? Who do these characters represent?

Characters can be studied in terms of how they are constructed. What kinds of words does Wilde use to describe characters? How do these word choices help readers understand how Wilde wants us to feel about and react to particular characters?

Sample Topics:

1. **The Happy Prince:** Is his treatment of the swallow fair, or is the Happy Prince exploiting the swallow with a full understanding that these actions will lead to the swallow's death?

   Is the Happy Prince self-sacrificing? Or is this impossible, since the prince is already dead, thus necessitating his use of the swallow to perform the actions? The prince has a literal change of heart, and one of the ironies of the tale is that once his heart is lead, he is finally able to love. Does anything about the prince's characterization suggest homosexual overtones? If you study Wilde's biography, are you able to find connections between Wilde's own life and his characterization of the prince?

2. **The swallow:** Is the swallow a true hero, acting out of altruism, or is he simply very naive?

In what ways is the swallow's spiritual journey similar to or different from the prince's spiritual journey? Does it appear that the swallow is making his own choices, or is he simply following wishes and instructions of the prince? What does the answer to this question reveal about the swallow's character? Why does Wilde choose to make this character a bird—specifically, a swallow? What kinds of people might the swallow represent?

3. **Mayor and town councillors:** What kinds of characteristics do the mayor and town councillors share?

What does this reveal about the ways in which the town is viewed and run? Which kinds of actual people might these characters represent? How can you tell? What are they really arguing about in their final scene? It seems that we cannot blame them completely for their reaction to the prince's statue—they just don't know the entire story. Does Wilde offer any suggestions for helping the mayor and town councillors become more like the swallow and the prince?

4. **Townspeople:** Do the townspeople learn and grow through the story? Why or why not? How can you tell?

Do the townspeople make any sacrifices or show mercy like the swallow and the prince do?

History and Context

Another fascinating approach to literature involves looking at the effects that a particular place and time period have on a work. It can be very enlightening to investigate who was the original audience for the work, what might have inspired Wilde to write it, what readers' reactions were to the story, and how many incarnations the story had in Wilde's time.

Wilde breaks one of the basic conventions of the fairy tale by allowing issues and elements of the real world to be addressed in the tale. Readers can recognize their own behaviors, problems, and societies in the town and its people. Which particular aspects of his own society and time period does Wilde appear to be addressing here?

Sample Topics:

1. **Samuel Johnson's *Rasselas*:** Does Johnson's work influence Wilde's fairy tale in explicit and subtle ways?

   Rasselas is a character of Johnson's who lives in the Happy Valley, completely isolated from anything that could possibly make him unhappy. Rasselas escapes the Happy Valley and searches for what he calls "the choice of life." Perhaps you can already see similarities between Johnson's work and Wilde's. Look carefully at Johnson's work, particularly in terms of its importance to 18th- and 19th-century literature and culture.

2. **Poverty:** What were Wilde's thoughts and feelings about poverty?

   Certainly class differences were an enormous issue in Victorian England, and Wilde himself struggled with finances periodically. Is *The Happy Prince* Wilde's indictment of government, or Victorian society, in terms of its lack of aid for the truly destitute? Does the fairy tale oversimplify the problems and solutions to poverty, or is Wilde's point possibly the idea that poverty could be fairly easily overcome if more people were willing to help?

Philosophy and Ideas

It is easy to write off Wilde's philosophies in *The Happy Prince* as sort of accidental outcomes that only occur because he is writing for children. A closer study of the tale, though, reveals Wilde's intentions more clearly. Wilde certainly wrote the fairy tales for children, and yet the genre was wildly popular in the late 19th century, and Wilde knew that adults would ready his fairy tales too. He writes for both audiences, allowing children to glean simple Golden Rule–type messages even as adults see more layers and are able to find more complex and sometimes controversial philosophies and ideas.

The Happy Prince and several other Wilde fairy tales stand out in his oeuvre as pieces that work against the aestheticism for which Wilde is still known. The fact is that Wilde's relationship with aesthetic philosophy was more complex than is often recognized. Regardless, tales like *The Happy Prince* make compelling studies because of the supposedly "mixed" messages throughout Wilde's work and because, much like all other aspects of Wilde's life and work, what we find on the surface is nowhere near the whole story.

Sample Topics:

1. **Hedonism:** Is *The Happy Prince* a rejection of hedonism?

   The pursuit of pleasure is a philosophy that Wilde is widely understood to have embraced. Yet *The Happy Prince* certainly does not promote pleasure. Rather, the fairy tale highlights the importance of sacrifice, attention, and kindness. Was Wilde talking out of both sides of his mouth, saying one thing and doing another? Is his anti-hedonism message one that he preaches only to children, even while sending the opposite message to adults? Or are we misreading Wilde's life and work by calling him a student and exemplar of hedonism?

2. **Aestheticism:** What does the tale, particularly the art professor character, convey about aestheticism?

   The Art Professor explains why the statue of the prince must be taken down: "As he is no longer beautiful he is no longer useful" (34). Throughout the tale Wilde makes a distinction between pleasure and happiness—the prince and the swallow both make choices that make them happy yet deny them some expected pleasures. Why does Wilde, who is regarded as a spokesperson for aestheticism, choose to speak against its precepts here? Why is Wilde's reputation more closely tied to aestheticism than to what some would regard as more morally substantive messages, like the one in *The Happy Prince*?

Form and Genre

Form and genre provide ways of classifying works that usually allow us to study them more fully. Form is defined as the style and structure of a work, whereas genre is the type, or classification, of a work. Both form and genre are usually distinct from a work's content, though writers use each of them quite specifically in order to convey a particular message, reach a certain audience, or to simply strengthen the impact of their work.

Form and genre are particularly complex issues for *The Happy Prince*: "in [Wilde's] letters he refers to the writing in *The Happy Prince* . . . as 'stories,' 'tales,' 'studies in prose,' 'fairy stories,' 'fairy tales,' and, once, as a 'collection of short stories'" (Tattersall 134). Carol Tattersall writes:

> They are studies in prose, put for Romance's sake into a fanciful form: meant partly for children and partly for those who have kept the childlike faculties of wonder and joy, and who find in simplicity a subtle strangeness. [They] are an attempt to mirror modern life in a form remote from reality—to deal with modern problems in a mode that is ideal and not imitative: I hope you will like them: they are, of course slight and fanciful, and written not for children, but for childlike people from eighteen to eighty! (135)

Wilde himself writes, "The story is an attempt to treat a tragic modern problem in a form that aims at delicacy and imaginative treatment: it is a reaction against the purely imitative character of modern art—and now that literature has taken to blowing loud trumpets I cannot but be pleased that some ear has cared to listen to the low music of a little reed" (*Letters* 221).

Sample Topic:

1. **Fairy tale:** What is the difference between fairy tales and fairy stories?

Wilde twice called the creations in *The Happy Prince* "studies in prose," "which suggests that they are indeed experimental: they combine the fantasy and the simplicity expected of the tale and the sophistication and complexity that have come to be associated with the short story" (Tattersall 135).

Language, Symbols, and Imagery

Writing about the language, symbols, and imagery within a literary work requires you to look specifically at how the work is constructed, as opposed to just studying the content of the work. Like many of the other elements in *The Happy Prince*, the language, symbols, and imagery in the story work on both adult and children's levels.

Pay particular attention to words, phrases, and repetition of words, phrases, and ideas in order to begin to see how Wilde uses language, symbols, and imagery. Summarizing the content may be necessary for illustrating particular points, but it is not the end product of this type of paper. You will want to look at things like syntax, word choice, and general diction. Do some characters speak differently than others? If so, why? Speech can be tied to all kinds of issues like economic class, education, geography, and stress, just to name a few. Discovering that two characters have distinct ways of speaking might lead you to research on economic classes and their respective educations, requiring some background in the historical context. Ultimately, you are looking at Wilde's choices as a writer and the possible reasons behind such choices.

Finding symbolism in a work involves looking for something that stands for something else. What kinds of things seem to be important to the tale and its characters? These things might be tangible objects like letters or particular foods, but they might also be something like a particular color associated with similar things throughout the work.

Imagery encapsulates things that can be perceived with our five senses: sight, sound, taste, smell, and touch. Are there elements of imagery that recur throughout the work, perhaps associated with specific characters, places, or activities? For example, is it always dark and dreary around a certain character, offering a clue to this character's disposition or lifestyle or the ways in which Wilde is asking us to perceive this character?

Sample Topics:

1. **"Adult imitation of childish thinking"** (Roditi 72): Is this a fair assessment of Wilde's language in *The Happy Prince*?

   How does Wilde's use of language help us to understand his intended audience as well as his intended messages? Many scholars, and even Wilde's youngest son, have mentioned Wilde's sometimes childish nature. How is this playfulness conveyed through the language, symbols, and imagery of this fairy tale?

2. **The number three:** What kinds of things happen in threes in the story?

   Why is the number three significant to the fairy tale form? What might the number three symbolize in *The Happy Prince*?

3. **Satire:** How can we tell when Wilde is writing satirically and when he is being serious?

   "There is a piquant touch of contemporary satire which differentiates Mr. Wilde from the teller of pure fairy tales; but it is so delicately introduced that the illusion is not destroyed and a child would delight in the tales without being worried or troubled by their application, while children of larger growth will enjoy them and profit by them" (Unsigned 60).

4. **Personification:** Why does not Wilde just write a story about people rather than giving human attributes to a statue and a bird?

   What effect does the personification of the reed have on readers? Are we to understand this as the swallow's foolish mistake, or is the reed humanized in this way to everyone?

Compare and Contrast Essays

Writing a paper that compares and/or contrasts elements of a text involves much more than simply listing similarities and differences between two or more things. These lists might help you early in the drafting process, but your paper eventually needs to go beyond this point to discuss why these similarities and/or differences are notable and important to the work. You would do well to ask questions like: Does Wilde intentionally set up some comparisons in order to perhaps show different points of view or circumstances? Do we notice particular comparisons and contrasts simply because of the time in which we live and our perceptions of the 19th century?

One of the most interesting things you can do with this type of paper is to make a comparison between two or more things/characters that on the surface seem very similar. The more surprising your comparison or contrast is, the more engaging your paper could be to your readers (provided you back yourself up with sufficient evidence from the text). You cannot make a comparison or contrast statement based solely on your own perceptions and "feelings" about the work. Whatever claim you decide to make must be supportable through the text itself.

Sample Topics:

1. ***The Happy Prince* and Wilde's other work:** How does *The Happy Prince* differ from Wilde's other work?

   You can compare and contrast *The Happy Prince* with several of Wilde's works to very different effect. Comparing the tale to Wilde's other fairy tales as opposed to comparing it to Wilde's plays or novel will clearly have very different results. Did Wilde seem to want *The Happy Prince* to stand out among his other work? Why or why not?

Bibliography for *The Happy Prince*

Killeen, Jarlath. "The Happy Prince." *The Fairy Tales of Oscar Wilde.* Hampshire: Ashgate, 2007. 21–40.

Martin, Robert K. "Oscar Wilde and The Fairy Tale: 'The Happy Prince' as Self-Dramatization." *Studies in Short Fiction* 16.1 (Winter 1979): 74–77.

Roditi, Edouard. *Oscar Wilde.* Norfolk: New Directions Books, 1947.

Shillinglaw, Ann. "Fairy Tales and Oscar Wilde's Public Charms." *Oscar Wilde: The Man, His Writings, and His World.* Ed. Robert N. Keane. New York: AMS Press, 2003. 81–91.

Tattersall, Carol. "An Immodest Proposal: Rereading Oscar Wilde's 'Fairy Tales.'" *Wascana Review* 26.1–2 (1991): 128–39.

Unsigned notice. *Athenaeum* (September 1, 1888) 286. *Oscar Wilde: The Critical Heritage.* Ed. Karl Beckson. New York: Barnes & Noble, 1970. 60.

Wilde, Oscar. *The Happy Prince.* 1888. *Oscar Wilde: The Major Works.* Ed. Isobel Murray. Oxford: Oxford UP, 2000. 28–35.

LADY WINDERMERE'S FAN

READING TO WRITE

*L*ADY WINDERMERE'S FAN was Oscar Wilde's first popular play. It was also the first time the playwright had paid so much attention to his work, both written and performed. Wilde began writing it in late 1890, early 1891, and it reached the stage in February 1892. He made changes even after its premiere, most notably making the audience aware of Mrs. Erylnne's true identity much earlier in the play.

After the first performance of *Lady Windermere's Fan,* the crowd called out for the writer, so Wilde got on stage and said, "Ladies and gentleman: I have enjoyed this evening immensely. The actors have given us a charming rendering of a delightful play, and your appreciation has been *most* intelligent. I congratulate you on the great success of your performance, which persuades me that you think almost as highly of the play as I do myself" (Pearson viii). Critics and scholars have interpreted this little speech in a number of ways, saying that it demonstrates Wilde's lack of respect for actors, for example, as he seems to take all of the credit for the play's performance. Others claim that the speech simply shows Wilde's fun, flamboyant, and rather shocking personality.

The play itself is not shocking, per se, although if Mrs. Erlynne had not rescued Lady Windermere from Lord Darlington's rooms it certainly might have become so. *Lady Windermere's Fan* is full of thoughtful, poignant, and intellectual phrases and ideas, right from the very beginning:

LADY WINDERMERE. [*Gravely.*] I hope not. I should be sorry to have
to quarrel with you, Lord Darlington. I like you very much, you know

that. But I shouldn't like you at all if I thought you were what most other men are. Believe me, you are better than most other men, and I sometimes think you pretend to be worse.

LORD DARLINGTON. We all have our little vanities, Lady Windermere.

LADY WINDERMERE. Why do you make that your special one? [*Still seated at table L.*]

LORD DARLINGTON. [*Still seated L.C.*] Oh, nowadays so many conceited people go about Society pretending to be good, that I think it shows rather a sweet and modest disposition to pretend to be bad. Besides, there is this to be said. If you pretend to be good, the world takes you very seriously. If you pretend to be bad, it doesn't. Such is the astounding stupidity of optimism.

LADY WINDERMERE. Don't you *want* the world to take you seriously then, Lord Darlington?

LORD DARLINGTON. No, not the world. Who are the people the world takes seriously? All the dull people one can think of, from the Bishops down to the bores. I should like *you* to take me very seriously, Lady Windermere, *you* more than any one else in life.

LADY WINDERMERE. Why—why me?

LORD DARLINGTON [*After a slight hesitation.*] Because I think we might be great friends. Let us be great friends. You may want a friend some day.

LADY WINDERMERE. Why do you say that?

LORD DARLINGTON. Oh—we all want friends at times.

LADY WINDERMERE. I think we're very good friends already, Lord Darlington. We can always remain so as long as you don't—

LORD DARLINGTON. Don't what?

LADY WINDERMERE. Don't spoil it by saying extravagant silly things to me. You think I am a Puritan, I suppose? Well, I have something of the Puritan in me. I was brought up like that. I am glad of it. My mother died when I was a mere child. I lived always with Lady Julia, my father's elder sister you know. She was stern to me, but she taught me, what the world is forgetting, the difference that there is between what is right and what is wrong. *She* allowed of no compromise. *I* allow of none.

LORD DARLINGTON. My dear Lady Windermere!

LADY WINDERMERE [*Leaning back on the sofa.*] You look on me as being behind the age.—Well, I am! I should be sorry to be on the same level as an age like this.

LORD DARLINGTON. You think the age very bad?

LADY WINDERMERE. Yes. Nowadays people seem to look on life as a speculation. It is not a speculation. It is a sacrament. Its ideal is Love. Its purification is sacrifice.

LORD DARLINGTON [*Smiling.*] Oh, anything is better than being sacrificed!

LADY WINDERMERE [*Leaning forward.*] Don't say that.

LORD DARLINGTON. I do say it. I feel it—I know it. (335-37)

One of the first things we get from this passage is Lady Windermere's tendency to make overgeneralizations, lumping "all men" or "people" together and trying to justify her assumptions based on fairly limited experience with people in general. You might want to write a paper focusing on Lady Windermere in order to study how she changes (or does not change) throughout the play. Be sure to ask how and why she changes or doesn't change in order to form some sort of argument, idea, or opinion of your own about the character and the play. Other questions about Lady Windermere include whether or not she is as old-fashioned as she claims to be. Does Wilde equate old-fashioned with closed-minded? Is old-fashioned rather something to be viewed as charming and innocent? Does Wilde use Lady Windermere's self-proclaimed old-fashioned nature to criticize the present age or to criticize the times before that? How can you tell?

Lord Darlington's character comes through very well in this early passage from the play, and perhaps we think we know him at this point. But look carefully at his words and think about his possible motivation. Is he bad or just pretending to be bad—a practice that he claims to find delightful? Are we to take him seriously? Do other characters take him seriously? Why or why not?

There are many more questions to be asked and answered about the play: Why, for example, does Wilde not allow Lady Windermere a reunion with her mother? Everyone else is allowed to know Mrs. Erlynne's identity. How would the play change if Lady Windermere were to learn the truth? You might even study the title of the play very carefully: *Lady Windermere's Fan: A Play about a Good Woman.* Look at the last lines of the play and ask, who exactly is the good woman of the title? Is Wilde being sarcastic? Ironic?

This play has been adapted into film several times. The first is a 1925 silent film, fascinating because it removes the heart of Wilde's wit and charm—the words. The most recent adaptation is a 2004 film titled *A Good Woman.* It is interesting that several film adaptations do not give Lady Windermere a child of her own, leaving us to speculate about such a choice. Why remove the child, who does not even actually appear in the play, but is only discussed? Why might it have been important to Wilde to make Lady Windermere a mother? Does eliminating the child change or remove any important plot points or subtleties of characterization?

TOPICS AND STRATEGIES

This section of the chapter addresses various possible topics for writing about *Lady Windermere's Fan* as well as general methods for approaching these topics. These lists are in no way exhaustive and are meant to provide a jumping-off point rather than an answer key. Use these suggestions to find your own ideas and form your own analyses. All topics discussed in this chapter could yield very effective papers.

Themes

It is important, when writing of a work's theme, to not only point out the overarching concept or idea that seems pervasive in the work but to discuss how and why this particular theme is important to the work. Perhaps the theme you have identified reveals something about the author's intentions, or maybe it highlights the role of an otherwise minor character. Whatever your conclusion, remember that the theme does something—gives a commentary of some kind—and therefore using your paper to point out its mere presence is not enough.

Sample Topics:

1. **Desperation:** Which characters are vengeful or predatory and which are simply desperate, or both?

Characters in *Lady Windermere's Fan* are in need of money, love, attention, and respectability, among other things. What does Wilde's work convey about each of these "needs"? Is desperation (or evil calculation) for certain things more acceptable than it is for other things? Which "needs" in the play are not met, and why?

2. **Love:** How do various characters in *Lady Windermere's Fan* define love?

Are some characters more capable of love than others? Why or why not? Does Wilde appear to differentiate between a mother's love for her child and a husband's love for his wife? If so, how? If not, how is it made clear to readers/theatergoers that all types of love are equal? Do characters in *Lady Windermere's Fan* only talk about love or do they demonstrate it as well? What, ultimately, seems to be the play's message about love? How can you tell?

3. **Betrayal:** Does Wilde seem to suggest that all betrayal is bad in some way, or is some measure of betrayal simply necessary?

In *Lady Windermere's Fan* there are characters who think they have been betrayed but have not, characters who are definitely being betrayed but do not suspect, and characters fully capable of justifying actions that to others appear to be betrayals. Which characters are most admirable and how involved are they in betraying someone else? What impact does our knowledge of their betrayal have on their characterization?

Character

Who is the good woman of the play's title? What role(s) do the men play? When you are studying a work in terms of characters, pay particular attention to character's actions or inaction. Which characters undergo some sort of change in the course of the play? Why or why not? You might also ask how the writer differentiates between characters. What makes Lord Darlington different from Lord Windermere, for example. Look carefully at all aspects of characterization: speech, dialect, dress, setting, symbolism, etc. Is there a character who is particularly associated with light or dark, for instance, and what does such an association reveal about Wilde's intentions for the character? Does a character seem to stand alone as a fully fictional being, or might he/she come to represent an actual person or group/type of people? How are characters regarded (by the playwright and/or other characters) and why? Investigate the methods of characterization as well. Do we learn about Lady Windermere, for example, through her own dialogue and description, or do we learn about her from others' observations and descriptions of her? There are many paths to follow here, including: manner of speaking (critics say that all of Wilde's characters sound the same. Is that true? Does it matter?), images/setting associated with a character, repeated words or phrases connected to a character, other characters' responses to a character, and the writer's commentary on a character.

Sample Topics:

1. **Lady Windermere:** To what degree is she following (or inclined to follow) in her mother's footsteps?

   Is she a good woman? Does she have better reasons for abandoning her child than Mrs. Erlynne did? Is she weak or strong (or somewhere in between)? Does she deserve to know that Mrs. Erlynne is her mother, or do the other characters do the right thing by keeping it from her? Why or why not? In what ways does Lady Windermere change through the course of the play? In what ways does she remain the same? How are her changes significant to her characterization and the play over-all? Does Wilde intend for readers/viewers to like Lady Wind-ermere? Why or why not? How can you tell?

2. **Mrs. Erlynne:** If she is the "good woman" that Lady Wind-ermere describes? Is she also bad or evil in some ways?

She makes several sacrifices—leaving her daughter in the first place, risking her reputation to save Lady Windermere's, not revealing herself to Lady Windermere. Yet she is also black-mailing Lord Windermere and seems to prefer her life outside the bonds of motherhood. Is she a victim of her time—forced to take extreme measures for any level of freedom? Does she simply lack some sort of maternal gene or instinct? Scholar Ann Heilmann writes, "One of the few truly transgressive women in Wilde's society dramas, Mrs. Erlynne is a female Dandy who *is* allowed a come-back at the end of the play" (141). What does the term *female Dandy* mean and how does it apply to Mrs. Erlynne? In what ways is she "truly transgressive," and what impact does that have on Wilde's characterization of her, readers' reactions to her, and our responses to events in the play?

3. **Lord Darlington:** What is his role, exactly?

Is he really in love with Lady Windermere, or is he a playboy with no serious intentions at all? Lord Darlington has some of the most memorable lines in the play, including one of Wilde's most famous: "We are all in the gutter, but some of us are look-ing at the stars." How does this line contribute to Wilde's char-acterization of Lord Darlington? Though Lord Darlington is not always taken seriously by other characters, it seems that in many ways he is the most practical, or level-headed, character in the play. Are his comments and predictions correct? Is he in some way the hero of the play? How so or why not?

History and Context

Many readers and scholars claim that Wilde wrote in a rather insulated way, with no time for social commentary or reform. Close readings of plays like *Lady Windermere's Fan,* however, reveal that Wilde is in fact writing social commentary and has much to criticize about class systems, judgments, and general attitudes, particularly those of the upper classes.

Writing about history and context requires you to look at a text in light of either the time in which it was written or the time in which the story is set. For Wilde these are one and the same. We should not underestimate the tricky nature of this setting for Wilde, considering that in *Lady Windermere's Fan* he criticizes some of the very people in the play's audience. Studying these aspects further can help you answer some very compelling questions: How did Wilde's contemporary audiences respond to a play that was in some ways about them? Why did Wilde choose to write *Lady Windermere's Fan* this way, rather than hiding his social commentary behind a different setting or context?

You might also write about Wilde's own life when thinking of the history and context of *Lady Windermere's Fan.* Do any of the characters represent/resemble people Wilde actually knew?

Sample Topics:

1. **Setting:** What messages about late 19th-century society does Wilde convey through setting in this play?

   The people attending *Lady Windermere's Fan* in the theater were precisely the society Wilde depicts in the play. The Windermere's home is only a short distance from the theater, and they operate in the same social and geographic circles as Wilde's audience. Why is it so important to Wilde to get the details of this setting correct? What reasons might he have for wanting to reach this particular type of audience with this play? Although the play is certainly critical of some aspects of upper-class society, it remains a desirable goal for characters to be a part of just this society. How does Wilde walk the fine line between criticism and respect?

2. **Stage/film presentations:** In what ways does Wilde's work endure and continue to resonate with audiences?

   Several adaptations of *Lady Windermere's Fan* were produced (and occasionally filmed) throughout the 20th and into the 21st centuries. How does the historical context of the adaptation affect Wilde's work? In other words, how do societal, political, and artistic issues of 1925 become reflected in Ernst Lubitsch's silent film version of *Lady Windermere's Fan*? Why is the 2004 film titled *A Good Woman* rather than *Lady Windermere's Fan*?

Philosophy and Ideas

Studying the philosophy and ideas behind a work provides us with opportunities for remarking on the larger picture surrounding the piece. To find the philosophy and ideas in *Lady Windermere's Fan*, look for the concepts that seem to pervade the entire play—in other words, the larger, world, or intellectual issues about which the play seems to comment. Sometimes you will find that a particular character is a sort of mouthpiece for a philosophy or an idea. Sometimes you will find groups of characters who seem to agree on these larger issues. Once you have identified one or more philosophies or ideas in a work it is important to ask questions and find something to say or argue about them, as simply pointing out their presence is usually not adequate. Ask yourself what Wilde seems to want to convey about a particular philosophy, for example. Does having a particular character "preaching" an idea show that Wilde himself wanted to promote the same idea, or is he putting these words into this character's mouth in order to make the idea look ridiculous or mean?

Sample Topics:

1. **Ethics:** Do characters in *Lady Windermere's Fan* demonstrate varying degrees of ethical responsibility?

   Is there a particular character whose actions or choices are particularly unethical? Why does Wilde write it this way? Lady Windermere, for example, is not necessarily unethical, but her views and judgments of others change fairly dramatically throughout the play. Do her views change because of her opinions of people's ethics have changed, or is it simply because she is still unaware of others' true character? It seems that Wilde's depiction of an ethical person is tied to the general description of an ethical person as "good." In that case, look for the characters in the play who are described as good. Who is describing them that way, and what impact does the descriptor's character have on the validity of the description? Does anyone seem to be regarded as better than others in some way? Why and how?

2. **Moral absolutism (absolute morality):** Does Lady Windermere practice the moral absolutism that she preaches?

Moral absolutism (or absolute morality) is the belief that certain actions are always right or wrong, no matter their context. There are, in other words, absolute, fixed standards based on morality. Find the lines that best express Lady Windermere's philosophies. How do other characters react? How does Wilde feel about these ideas? How can you tell? What message does Wilde want readers to get about moral absolutism? Why? How can you tell?

Form and Genre

Form and genre provide ways of classifying works that usually allow us to study them more fully. Form is defined as the style and structure of a work, whereas genre is the type, or classification, of a work. Both form and genre are usually distinct from a work's content, though writers use each of them quite specifically in order to convey a particular message, reach a certain audience, or to simply strengthen the impact of their work.

Wilde uses very conventional, traditional, recognizable devices and motifs: lady concealed in a man's room (not her husband's), mislaid fan, long-lost child/parent, rival women, misdirected letter, scene of discovery. But he almost always puts a new spin on the conventional form (nothing is actually learned by Lady Windermere in the scene of discovery; the parent [not child] is lost, but never "found" in the sense traditionally used, etc.) (Peckham 11–12). In what ways do these unconventional uses of devices and motifs surprise the audience?

Sample Topics:

1. **Social comedy:** How can we tell when Wilde is making a sincere point, and when he is simply trying to get a laugh?

This genre would become Wilde's best known. How does the genre allow him to mix drama with comedy, criticism with humor? Wilde is still largely known as a funny, rather harmless writer, though scholars have read his works for their social commentary and have recently begun reading for Wilde's more serious underpinnings—his ideas and pushes for social change/reform. Does *Lady Windermere's Fan* do more than poke fun at a particular class of people? What does Wilde appear to be criticizing? Advocating?

2. **Melodrama:** Does the play (and/or its characters) seem one-dimensional?

Melodramas tend to be formulaic and fairly one-dimensional. Wilde certainly uses well-known formulas in *Lady Windermere's Fan*, but he generally alters them at least a little so that they do not quite meet readers' standard expectations. In other words, are there nuances in the plot and within the characters that show us that they are not wholly good or entirely evil, etc.? In what ways might Wilde be using the play to poke fun at melodrama? Think, for example, of Lady Windermere in the first scenes. Her world is pretty clear-cut, and she seems to believe that people are fairly one-dimensional. Does Wilde support her worldview in the play or do other characters and actions undercut Lady Windermere's assumptions?

Language, Symbols, and Imagery

Studying a work for language, symbols, and imagery requires careful attention to not only the words themselves but the scenes and people they depict. For a play like *Lady Windermere's Fan*, you might look closely at the ways in which characters speak. Do particular words and/or accents garner positive or negative attention? How do characters describe one another, and what does this reveal about both characters involved? Does Wilde use particular words to describe or relate to a setting or character? Why? What kind of atmosphere or characterization does such word choice create?

Symbols are important in literature, allowing us to see one thing with the understanding that it represents something else. Think of the title of this play. Could Lady Windermere's fan be a symbol of something? Her relationship with her husband? Her "goodness" as a human being? Her reputation as a lady? Study what happens to the fan and see if your idea for the fan as a symbol holds up through the action of the play. If the fan symbolizes the Windermeres' marriage, for example, what does it mean when Lady Windermere leaves the fan at Lord Darlington's? What can we conclude from the fact that Mrs. Erlynne ends up possessing the fan at the end? Look for objects of significance in the play, decide what you think they symbolize, and then follow that symbolism to its logical conclusion to see if it holds up through the action of the entire play.

Imagery involves the detail of the play—the part that readers can grasp with one or more of their five senses. What kind of atmosphere is created during the Windermeres' party, for example? Are you able to feel like you can clearly see and hear the people? Why or why not?

Sample Topics:

1. **Irony/dramatic irony:** Does Wilde seem to want to frustrate readers by giving them more information than some of the characters?

   The audience knows that Mrs. Erlynne is Lady Windermere's mother, but Lady Windermere never does. Does this make us feel sorry for Lady Windermere? What effect does this irony have on readers? Characters? If you were to write an additional act for *Lady Windermere's Fan,* would you reveal Mrs. Erlynne's identity to Lady Windermere? Why or why not? The play's first performance kept Mrs. Erlynne's identity a secret until act four. After the audience's significant confusion on the first night, Wilde moved the revelation of Mrs. Erlynne's identity to act two, where it remains today.

2. **Payments, buying, and selling:** Who or what is bought and/or sold in the play, and what are the (literal and figurative) costs?

   Buying and selling are both spoken of in literal or pithy ways in the play, but these actions symbolize the costs of appearances, honor, and sacrifice. What does all of this commodification assume or reveal about upper-class society? Do any characters hold things sacred, not ever considering buying or selling them?

3. **Roses:** Why did Wilde find roses important enough to make them the end of Lady Windermere's conversation with her husband?

The roses Lady Windermere speaks of at the end of the play are white and red, very clear-cut colors, no in-between shades of pink. Are such clearly defined colors somehow a symbol for Lady Windermere and her clearly delineated ideas about people? Might red symbolize evil or the devil while white symbolizes purity and innocence? Despite her claims and speeches, Lady Windermere still has clear categories in her life—she has never questioned the basis by which she judges people, and the symbolic colors of the roses reveal that (Peckham). Red could also symbolize the blood ties between Lady Windermere and Mrs. Erlynne.

Compare and Contrast Essays

It is usually easy to find elements of a literary work to hold up for comparison and/or contrast. It is considerably more challenging (and therefore more rewarding) to not only point out similarities and differences between characters or elements in the work but to investigate why those similarities and differences are important to the literature.

Comparisons and contrasts are often more interesting and fun if the pairing is unexpected. Lady Windermere and Mrs. Erlynne are probably worth some consideration in terms of comparisons and contrasts, but the pairing is fairly obvious. What about Lord Darlington and Lord Windermere? Are they more alike than they are different? If so, how? If not, is one of them the clear hero, the other a likely villain?

Be sure to consider the larger questions involved in your comparison and/or contrast. What effect does such a pairing/grouping have on the work as a whole, on readers' responses to the work, on the writer's apparent intentions for the work, etc.?

1. **Agatha and Lady Windermere:** The title of the play contains Lady Windermere's name, but in some ways is Agatha a more important character?

What is Agatha's role in this play, exactly? It seems apparent that audiences are supposed to like Lady Windermere, at least to some degree. Are audiences also supposed to like Agatha? Why or why not? How does comparing and contrasting these two characters help us to understand the degree to which the play itself focuses on women?

2. **High culture and mass/consumer culture:** Is there really a big difference between the two?

Which aspect/section of culture does Wilde seem to be critiquing most heavily? Why? How can you tell? Which characters represent each aspect of culture? How do the characters' personalities and interactions help us to understand Wilde's point about both high culture and consumer culture? In what ways did Wilde's own life reflect important participation in both of these types of culture?

Bibliography for *Lady Windermere's Fan*

Heilmann, Ann. "Wilde's New Women: The New Woman on Wilde." *The Importance of Reinventing Oscar: Versions of Wilde during the Last 100 Years.* Eds. Uwe Böker, Richard Corballis, and Julie A. Hibbard. Amsterdam: Rodopi, 2002. 135–46.

Pearson, Hesketh. Introduction. *Five Plays.* By Oscar Wilde. New York: Bantam Books, 1961. vii–xvi.

Peckham, Morse. "What Did Lady Windermere Learn?" *College English* 18.1 (Oct. 1956).

Wilde, Oscar. *Lady Windermere's Fan.* 1892. Ed. *Oscar Wilde: The Major Works.* Isobel Murray. Oxford: Oxford World's Classics, 1989. 331–88.

SALOMÉ

READING TO WRITE

THERE ARE at least 13 stage and screen versions of *Salomé* based on Wilde's version, including a wildly popular opera by Richard Strauss. As of this writing, Al Pacino is writing and directing *Salomaybe?*, a feature-film combination of "documentary, fiction, and improvisation" that "unravels and reinterprets" *Salomé.* There are a number of versions of the biblical story out there: "The Salomes of Flaubert, of Moreau, Laforque and Mallarmé are known only to students of literature and connoisseurs, but the *Salomé* of the genial comedian Wilde is known to all the world" (Prax 337). Wilde likely had several influences—the Bible, J. K. Huysmans's 1884 novel *À Rebours,* and paintings by Gustave Moreau—but the tale and characters in his play are still largely fictional conglomerations and inventions.

One interesting question to ask about this play is whether it is Wilde's only serious play. Wilde himself called the play a tragedy, reminding us of the work's subtitle: *A Tragedy in One Act.* Whatever you decide about the genre of the play, it seems that the circumstances surrounding the play's production certainly were tragic. *Salomé* was produced in Paris while Wilde was in prison. Rehearsals actually began in 1892, but in June the Examiner of Plays for the Lord Chamberlain would not license the play because of its biblical basis. An unsigned review of the play seems to agree with Lord Chamberlain: "It is an arrangement in blood and ferocity, morbid, *bizarre,* repulsive, and very offensive in its adaptation of scriptural phraseology to situations the reverse of sacred" (8). Do audiences/readers today find the play offensive? Why or why not?

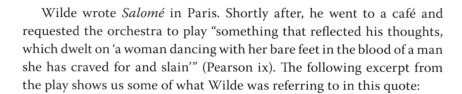

Wilde wrote *Salomé* in Paris. Shortly after, he went to a café and requested the orchestra to play "something that reflected his thoughts, which dwelt on 'a woman dancing with her bare feet in the blood of a man she has craved for and slain'" (Pearson ix). The following excerpt from the play shows us some of what Wilde was referring to in this quote:

> Ah! thou wouldst not suffer me to kiss thy mouth, Iokanaan. Well! I will kiss it now. I will bite it with my teeth as one bites a ripe fruit. Yes, I will kiss thy mouth, Iokanaan. I said it; did I not say it? I said it. Ah! I will kiss it now. . . . But wherefore dost thou not look at me, Iokanaan? Thine eyes that were so terrible, so full of rage and scorn, are shut now. Wherefore are they shut? Open thine eyes! Lift up thine eyelids, Iokanaan! Wherefore dost thou not look at me? Art thou afraid of me, Iokanaan, that thou wilt not look at me? . . . And thy tongue, that was like a red snake darting poison, it moves no more, it speaks no words, Iokanaan, that scarlet viper that spat its venom upon me. It is strange, is it not? How is it that the red viper stirs no longer? . . . Thou wouldst have none of me, Iokanaan. Thou rejectedst me. Thou didst speak evil words against me. Thou didst bear thyself toward me as to a harlot, as to a woman that is a wanton, to me, Salome, daughter of Herodias, Princess of Judea! Well, I still live, but thou art dead, and thy head belongs to me. I can do with it what I will. I can throw it to the dogs and to the birds of the air. That which the dogs leave, the birds of the air shall devour. . . . Ah, Iokanaan, Iokanaan, thou wert the man that I loved alone among men! All other men were hateful to me. But thou wert beautiful! They body was a column of ivory set upon feet of silver. It was a garden full of doves and lilies of silver. It was a tower of silver decked with shields of ivory. There was nothing in the world so white as thy body. There was nothing in the world so black as thy hair. In the whole world there was nothing so red as thy mouth. Thy voice was a censer that scattered strange perfumes, and when I looked on thee I heard a strange music. Ah! wherefore didst thou not look at me, Iokanaan? With the cloak of thine hands, and with the cloak of thy blasphemies thou didst hide thy face. Thou didst put upon thine eyes the covering of him who would see his God. Well, thou hast seen thy God, Iokanaan, but me, me, thou didst never see. If thou hadst seen me thou hadst loved me. I saw thee, and I loved thee. Oh, how I loved thee! I love thee yet, Iokanaan. I love only thee. . . . I am athirst for thy beauty; I am

hungry for thy body; and neither wine nor apples can appease my desire. What shall I do now, Iokanaan? Neither the floods nor the great waters can quench my passion. I was a princess, and thou didst scorn me. I was a virgin, and thou didst take my virginity from me. I was chaste, and thou didst fill my veins with fire. . . . Ah! ah! wherefore didst thou not look at me? If thou hadst looked at me thou hadst loved me. Well I know that thou wouldst have loved me, and the mystery of Love is greater than the mystery of Death. (327–28)

Why is the image of Salomé's kiss so violent? There is actually a lot of violent imagery in this speech: biting Iokanaan's lips, "red snake darting poison," venom, death, and devouring, to identify just a few examples. How does this passage help us to characterize Salomé? What does Wilde seem to want us to understand about her?

Do you think that Salomé really believes her own words? She speaks of her love for Iokanaan, and how she has never felt this way before. Were "all men" really always hateful to her before? What has Iokanaan done that is different? How much of the situation lives in Salomé's imagination?

At the end of her speech, Salomé seems to equate love with death. How does this equation ring true throughout the rest of the play? What does this reveal? One cannot love without risking death? Does love seem to cause death directly?

TOPICS AND STRATEGIES

This section of the chapter addresses various possible topics for writing about *Salomé* as well as general methods for approaching these topics. These lists are in no way exhaustive and are meant to provide a jumping-off point rather than an answer key. Use these suggestions to find your own ideas and form your own analyses. All topics discussed in this chapter could turn into very effective papers.

Themes

There are several themes in *Salomé* and an equal number of contradicting interpretations of those themes. What, for example, does the play convey about religion? Wilde scholar Christopher Nassaar claims that "Instead of Christianity, Wilde builds and aesthetic mythological religion of evil around the cruel moon goddess Cybele and her incarnation on earth, the Princess Salome, and he presents himself as the antichrist of the Victorian period" (Nassaar "Wilde's" 35).

To write about a theme you want to think about general ideas or concepts in the work that stand out to you as particularly important. Look for these themes not only in the body of the text (especially in repeated words and phrases) but also in chapter titles or, in this case, stage directions. Once you have pinpointed a theme that you find compelling, go back through the text to try to determine what the writer and/or characters are trying to communicate about this theme. It is not enough to write that "Oscar Wilde writes about lust" and then summarize the play. Ask what Wilde is saying in particular about lust, and why. What do various characters do or say concerning lust, and how does this influence readers' feelings toward the character(s)? What clues can you find in stage directions concerning Wilde's attitude or intentions concerning lust in the play? Mere identification of a theme is not enough, so asking further questions will get you on your way to finding an effective point of claim about the play.

Sample Topics:

1. **Transgressive sexuality:** What does Wilde seem to want audiences to know about transgressive sexuality? How can we tell?

   Salomé desires Iokanaan and Herod desires Salomé. Salomé is active, even masculine, in her desire for Iokanaan, which directly threatens the patriarchy (i.e., Herod). Does her masculine demeanor and activity uncover some homoerotic tendencies in the play? What can we make of the supposed tradition of casting a girl as the page of Herodias and sometimes the Syrian? This casting certainly adds a homoerotic flavor to the play. Is this what Wilde intended, or is it a result of readers' and performers' assumptions and stereotypes regarding what Wilde may have wanted to convey?

2. **Religion:** Is Wilde "an atheist and an aesthetic Satanist" (Nassaar "Wilde's" 35)?

   Fictional though it may be, Wilde's play cannot escape its biblical bases entirely. What commentary does the play seem to demonstrate through Wilde's characterization of Iokanaan? Herod? Salomé? If you choose to argue that Wilde intends and makes no particularly religious comment, you must ask why he chooses to remove religious argument from an ultimately biblical story. Throughout Wilde's life he fluctuated between devotion/attraction to religion and resistance to religion. Are his personal religious questions and convictions reflected in the play? If so, how? If not, why not, and what is meant by the absence?

3. **Human nature:** In regard to the characters in this play, what are the fundamental aspects of human nature?

In *Salomé* Wilde explores the depths of human nature, demonstrating the blackness in Salomé's soul and the general depravity of the world around her. Does Wilde seem to find anything redeemable in human nature? Is there a greater good in this play?

Character

Are all the characters in *Salomé* essentially selfish? What kinds of things do they stand for and believe in? Are we supposed to like any of them? Why or why not? How can we tell?

Do any characters learn and grow? Which characters are we supposed to like? Why? How can we tell?

Christopher Nassaar writes: "Wilde's treatment of the story of Salome is not only original but also blasphemous, presenting her as a symbol of uninhibited human nature, embodying the gospel of total sexual liberation and willing to lose her life for it. She is decadence personified and yet offered to the Victorians within a religious framework" ("Pater's" 81).

In what ways are Wilde's characterizations true to the biblical accounts of this story? In what ways does he expand, elaborate, and even exaggerate?

How does Wilde write characters so that readers know that he intends them to be evil, or good, or somewhere in-between? What clues to characterization can you find in word choices, tone, or stage directions?

One way to study character in literature is to look at ways in which a character develops or does not develop through the course of the work.

Do any characters in *Salomé* learn and grow from their experiences? How so? What effect does this have on readers, on the plot, on the longevity of the play, etc.? Why might it be important in this play for some characters to remain constant rather than developing and changing? Often when writing about character, you want to keep a tight focus on only one or two characters.

Why does Wilde introduce characters who are not even mentioned in the Bible? What purpose does the page of Herodias serve, for example?

Sample Topics:

1. **Salomé:** To what extent is she both or either the victim and the aggressor?

   She possesses some generally masculine characteristics: "she is outspoken, strong-willed, even violent, and certainly reluctant to submit to the ultimate authority" (Gurfinkel 171). In what ways does Salomé represent or embody women of the Aesthetic Movement? Why does she want Iokanaan's head, and what does this desire reveal about her character? Is her request rational, reasonable?

2. **Herod:** How does Salomé's request put his superstition and his cruelty in conflict with one another?

   In what ways is Herod's character shaped by his actions and attitudes toward other characters? In what ways is Herod's character shaped by others' actions and attitudes toward him? What point does Wilde seem to be making about Herod? Why? How can you tell? Does Herod ever emerge as a kind of hero? Why or why not?

3. **Herodias:** Does she try to protect and help Salomé or use her for selfish gain?

   What are her motivations—jealousy? Motherly love? Altruism? Feminism? Does Herodias's role in the Bible story and in Wilde's play change or remain the same? How much influence over Salomé does she actually have?

4. **Iokanaan:** Is Wilde's character recognizable as John the Baptist? If so, how? If not, why not?

Does Wilde seem to want us to sympathize with Iokanaan? How can we tell? Does Wilde's characterization of Iokanaan reveal a perspective that comes from a particular religious affiliation? Is he "an example of sexual repression," as Wilde scholar Christopher Nassaar claims ("Wilde's" 35)? In what ways does Wilde's characterization of Iokanaan reveal Wilde's feelings about religion?

History and Context

In the case of *Salomé*, it is equally compelling to investigate the history and context of the play's content and the history and context of the play's debut, publications, and performances.

Wilde's version of *Salomé* is widely regarded as the most commonly known version of John the Baptist's beheading. Why? What other versions of this story exist? Why is it both appropriate and ironic for Wilde to be using a story from the Bible as inspiration? How does the story's biblical foundation complicate and/or simplify its themes and effectiveness?

A paper on history and context might focus on characters and the feelings and lifestyle they all seem to share. Clearly attitudes toward power (monarchy) and religion are different now. Is Wilde expressing attitudes of characters from biblical times, or do his characters become mouthpieces for Victorian attitudes and behaviors? How can you tell? However you answer these questions, think about what Wilde's intentions might have been.

Sample Topics:

1. **The biblical version:** What impact does the biblical version of the story have on Wilde's play?

Salomé's story is very brief in both the 14th chapter of Matthew and the sixth chapter of Mark. What does Wilde add to the story? Why? Do his additions and interpretations seem fair, or do they somehow change fundamental aspects of the original version? What in Wilde's own life inspired him to use a biblical story as inspiration?

2. **Sarah Bernhardt:** Was the play written for her, or at least with her in mind?

After her introduction to the play, Bernhardt committed to putting it on at the Palace Theatre in London. A very famous French actress, she was, incidentally, buried in the same Paris cemetery as Wilde. Conduct some research on Bernhardt to learn more about her life, her career, and her acting style. Why did Wilde choose her for Salomé? What might she have done with the role? Consider that she was known in part for her voice, and while all of the films she made are silent, there are recordings made of her voice. You might begin your research with Bernhardt's memoir, *My Double Life.*

3. **Censorship:** In what way does *Salomé* provide important lessons about censorship in Wilde's time?

Salomé was banned by the Lord Chamberlain because the law did not allow biblical subjects on stage in England. Wilde and actress Sarah Bernhardt were both furious, as the play had already been in rehearsal for three weeks. Wilde threatened to become a French citizen, striking out about censorship and morality, but the press mostly made fun of him. *Salomé* was published (in France first) in 1893 but was not performed until 1896, when Wilde was in prison. *Salomé* was staged first in Paris and then Berlin, not reaching London until 1905, five years after Wilde's death (Pearson ix).

Philosophy and Ideas

Studying the philosophy and ideas behind a work provides us with opportunities for remarking on the larger picture surrounding the piece. To find the philosophy and ideas in *Salomé,* look for the concepts that seem to pervade the entire play—in other words, the larger, world, or intellectual issues about which the play seems to comment. Sometimes you will find that a particular character is a sort of mouthpiece for a philosophy or an idea. Sometimes you will find groups of characters who seem to agree on these larger issues. Once you have identified one or more philosophies or ideas in a work it is important to ask questions and find something to say or argue about them, as simply pointing out their presence is usually not adequate. Ask yourself what Wilde seems to want to convey about a particular philosophy, for example. Does having a particular character "preaching" an idea show that Wilde himself wanted to promote the same idea, or is he putting these words into this character's mouth in order to make the idea look ridiculous or mean?

Sample Topic:

1. **Feminism:** To what degree can Salomé be considered a feminist play?

In some ways it seems that Wilde is attacking women in the play, even while highlighting women's power, emotion, and logic, and their influence on the world around them. Should Salomé have been given more power in the household or even the government? Would this have prevented her rather desperate action as the play progresses? Which events in the play seem particularly gender related? Why? How can you tell?

Form and Genre

In what ways does the form of *Salomé* demonstrate that even in a biblically based tale of murder, Wilde is not taking his play completely seriously?

Is the play too short? What might Wilde have done with *Salomé* if he had written another couple of acts? Why did he choose to write it as a one-act play?

Form and genre help us to categorize literary works in ways that make them easier to discuss. A work's form is its style and structure (epic, tragedy, romance, etc.), while its genre is its classification based on particular criteria (biography, mystery, adventure, etc.). Form and genre can be studied apart from a work's content, to some extent, so you want to avoid simply summarizing a work in attempt to verify a point about form or genre. It is crucial to consider that form and genre do not occur by accident, so looking at it in terms of the writer's choices becomes paramount. The work did not write itself, and chances are the writer was making very deliberate decisions in order to reach and affect a certain audience in particular ways.

Sample Topics:

1. **Opera liberetto:** What is it about the play that lends itself to musical performance and interpretation?

   This opinion is held by some but widely contested, as the play stands on its own without this categorization. Richard Strauss's operatic version of the play certainly adds to the musically oriented readings of *Salomé*. Strauss's opera became widely popular and no doubt helped to popularize Wilde's play as well.

2. **Drama:** Is *Salomé* a straightforward drama, or does it also contain elements of comedy and melodrama?

   Salomé certainly falls nicely into the drama genre. Wilde very nearly creates something new here, though he combines biblical language (*Iokanaan*) with everyday language, all tied up in a general Shakespearean package. The form of *Salomé* indicated by the language and the mix of old biblical tale and new fiction is innovative and original.

3. **Parody:** How do we know when Wilde is making fun of his characters?

   There is something tongue-in-cheek about Wilde's writing here. He certainly uses dark humor, as many readers smile when reading Herod's excessive speech about what he will give to Salomé. Does Wilde parody all of the action and characters, or are some treated with complete seriousness? Salomé's death, for example, is a parody of Isolda's death of love at the end of Wagner's opera *Tristan & Isolda*.

Language, Symbols, and Imagery

Studying language, symbols, and imagery in a work allows you to look beyond the work's content to see *how* the work is written. What choices has the writer made and why? Avoid lengthy plot summaries here and focus instead on how the writer's work achieves particular effects.

Language means much more than a classification of English, Spanish, French, etc. Studying language draws you in to elements like word choice, syntax, and general diction. How do various characters speak, and in what ways do their speech patterns affect readers' responses to them? You might also investigate language used by the writer or other characters to describe a particular character. Is there a lot of repetition and overlap in the ways that various characters describe Salomé, for example? What effect do such descriptions have on the play itself and/or readers' responses to it? Another tactic for studying language is to identify the tone or mood of the play, scene, character, or setting. How does Wilde use language to convey this tone or mood, and why is it significant?

Symbols in literature are essentially things that stand for something else. How can we tell, for example, that the moon in *Salomé* stands for something other than itself? What does it stand for, and why is this symbolism important for the play, the scene, the characters, or the setting?

Imagery involves elements of the work that can be perceived with one or more of the readers' five senses. Can we taste the blood as Salomé kisses Iokanaan? Why is this imagery important? What does Wilde seem particularly interested in making sure readers experience with their senses? This element can be particularly interesting to study in a play, where the writer's stage directions can offer additional clues and emphasis.

Sample Topics:

1. **Salomé symbolizes lust:** How can she symbolize lust and yet remain pure and innocent, as Wilde insisted she was?

   Wilde scholar Christopher Nassaar posits that Salomé is "a symbol of human nature but completely vampiric and evil" ("Wilde's" 35). Does Salomé symbolize lust? Human nature? Innocence? Does she somehow represent all of these things?

2. **Salomé's dance:** What does the dance in general, and the dance of the seven veils in particular, add to the play?

   Wilde appears to have invented the dance of the seven veils. Why? It gets the briefest mention, in terms of stage direction, so why does it take on such importance? Why does Wilde leave it wide open for actresses and directors to interpret? What does the dance come to represent for Salomé, other characters, and/or the plot in general?

3. **Musicality:** What is it about this play that makes it more rhythmic and musical than the average play?

The musicality of the speech in the play refers to high (Salomé) to low (Iokanaan) tones, as well as quiet conversations (Narraboth and the page) to shouts of the soldiers. In his journal *The Spirit Lamp*, Bosie wrote: "One thing strikes one very forcibly in the treatment, the musical form of it. Again and again it seems to one that in reading one is *listening*; listening, not to the author, not to the direct unfolding of a plot, but to the tones of different instruments, suggesting, suggesting always indirectly, till one feels that by shutting one's eyes one can best catch the suggestion" (21). Richard Strauss made *Salomé* a significant work of opera in the 20th century.

4. **The moon:** Which statements about the moon give us hints about the action to come?

Many characters make statements and observations about the moon. What is revealed about each character through his or her relationship with (opinion of) the moon? Why do so many statements about the moon contradict each other? The first dialogue in the play refers to Salomé and the moon in ways that make it difficult to tell which the characters refer to with the pronoun *she*. Then Salomé comes outside and seems to be talking about herself when she says: "How good to see the moon! She is like a little piece of money, a little silver flower. She is cold and chaste. I am sure she is a virgin. She has the beauty of a virgin. Yes, she is a virgin. She has never defiled herself. She has never abandoned herself to men, like the other goddesses" (304).

Compare and Contrast Essays

Comparing and contrasting does what it says it does—allows you to find similarities and differences in a work in order to comment on them. The cardinal rule of compare and contrast essays is to avoid simply making a list of similarities and/or differences. You must follow your points up with interpretation, invoking larger issues through analysis.

Sample Topics:

1. **Wilde's play and the film versions:** What parts of Wilde's play remain recognizable in the film versions?

   Certainly written works adapted for film always undergo changes. Do filmmakers keep many details the same? Do the films retain an essence or mood from Wilde's play? Three well-known film versions include the silent film from 1923, the 1953 version starring Rita Hayworth, and 1987's *Salomé's Last Dance*, which tells a story of Wilde himself alongside the story of Salomé. In what ways do these films reflect the ideologies and artistic techniques of their times? How does this help us to understand the ways in which Wilde's play reflects late Victorian ideologies and artistic techniques?

2. ***Salomé* and *Hamlet*:** What would Hamlet have done in Salomé's situation? What would Salomé have done in Hamlet's?

   Both plays center around royal characters whose mothers married their uncles, and the political, moral, and personal issues that result. Is that where the similarities end, or are there more connections between Wilde's work and Shakespeare's? Most readers understand Hamlet to hold noble motivations, even for gruesome actions, based on his love for his father. Does Salomé have similarly noble motivations? If we can posit that Hamlet may be insane, can we argue to same about Salomé?

3. **Religion and government:** What kinds of contrasts does the play present between religion and government?

   Does Wilde seem to be promoting one over the other, or are they equally desirable or detestable? Does the play convey particular aspects or types of religion and government, or is the commentary aimed at the institutions as a whole? Herod confuses Caesar with God or Jesus more than once and calls Caesar "lord of the world" and "lord of all things" (319). Does this confusion serve only to make Herod look ridiculous, or does it illustrate an overlap or greater confusion about religion and government?

Bibliography for *Salomé*

Douglas, Lord Alfred. "Salomé." *The Spirit Lamp* 4.1 (May 4, 1893): 21–27.

Gurfinkel, Helena. "'Yet Each Man Kills the Thing He Loves': Murder & Sexual Transgression in *The Importance of Being Earnest,* 'Lord Arthur Savill's Crime,' and *Salomé.*" *Oscar Wilde: The Man, His Writings, & His World.* Ed. Robert N. Keane. New York: Arms Press, 2003. 163–74.

Nassaar, Christopher. "Pater's *The Renaissance* & Wilde's *Salomé.*" *Explicator* 59.2 (Jan. 2001): 80–82.

———. "Wilde's *The Picture of Dorian Gray* & *Salomé.*" *Explicator* 57.1 (Oct. 1998): 33–35.

Praz, Mario. *The Romantic Agony.* 1966. Reprint, Oxford: Oxford UP, 1978.

Unsigned notice. "Salomé." *The Times* (23 Feb. 1893): 8.

Wilde, Oscar. *Salomé.* 1893. *Oscar Wilde: The Major Works.* Ed. Isobel Murray. Oxford: Oxford UP, 2000. 299–330.

INDEX